"A Lovely Letter From Cecie"

The 1907–1915 Vancouver Diary and World War I Letters of Wallace Chambers

by

John Graham Gillis

Canadian Cataloguing in Publication Data
Chambers, Wallace, 1886–1915.
"A lovely letter from Cecie"
ISBN 0-89716-815-1
1. Chambers, Wallace, 1886–1915. 2. Vancouver (B.C.)--
Biography. 3. World War, 1914–1918--Personal narratives,
Canadian. I. Gillis, John Graham, 1925– II. Title.
FC3847.26.C52A3 1998   971.1'3303'092   C98-910344-7
F1089.5.V22C52 1998

Editor: Suzanne Bastedo
Text Design: Fiona Raven
Cover Design: Andrew Johnstone

First printing May 1998

PEANUT BUTTER PUBLISHING
Suite 212 - 1656 Duranleau Street • Granville Island
• Vancouver, B.C. V6H 3S4 • 604-688-0320 •
301-Pier 55, 1101 Alaskan Way • Seattle, WA 98101-2982
• 206-748-0345 •
e mail: pnutpub@aol.com
Internet: http://www.pbpublishing.com

Printed in Canada

Table of Contents

Preface

~

On her twenty-fifth birthday, July 7, 1915, my mother, Gertie, heard the news that her only brother, Lieutenant Wallace Chambers, had been killed in action. The fact that sixty thousand other Canadian families would join them in shedding tears for lost ones in that horrible war did not assuage the grief of Gertie and her three sisters.

Ten years later, I was born. Four daughters had blessed the home before me, the first when Gertie was the age of her brother when he died — twenty-nine. In the mid-1960s, I received my Uncle Wallace's military box containing his 72nd Highlanders tam, cummerbund, spurs, bayonet, photos and diaries. These had been stored for decades by my Aunt Sue (Townley). I feel privileged to be their custodian.

I found Wallace's entries in the Vancouver diary as captivating as I found his letters from the trenches and battlefields dramatic and poignant. From the first time I read his diary, I was gripped by its eloquence, despite its being terse, even telegraphic. What was *not* said became meaningful too, like a musical composition with silent pauses between notes. It took the curtain off the post-Victorian attitudes and habits of young people in pre-

World War I Vancouver, and disclosed a specific idealistic mindset butchered by the nightmarish reality of a vicious war. Throughout the diary, I watched a twenty-year-old youth growing into adulthood. Wallace's early entries were those of an outgoing and energetic young person. His diary recorded that he filled each day with as many activities as he could, whether social, cultural, outdoor, or romantic. As the years progressed, his level of activity remained high, but what he wrote became more thoughtful, more detailed, and more concerned with hopes and dreams as he started to build his adult life. Wallace showed every promise of becoming a fine man. A tender love story also unfolded in his diary, and became a dominant theme as Wallace gradually fell in love with the woman with whom he had been corresponding since they met in 1905.

I believe that this book and the papers on which it is based have value as historical documents. To me, the richness, indeed the very soul of our culture, is made up largely of the past. And it is people who make up the tapestry of the past. Not just famous people, but ordinary people like my Uncle Wallace, with their feelings, goals, and strivings.

In addition to the diaries and letters which I have received, I am most grateful for another resource passed on to me by my Aunt Sue before she died: *History of the 16th Battalion (The Canadian Scottish): Canadian Expeditionary Force in the Great War, 1914–1919,* by H.M. Urquart, D.S.O., M.C., A.D.C. (The MacMillan Company of Canada, Limited, St. Martin's House, 1932). Another valuable resource which I must acknowledge is the Vancouver Archives.

I am also grateful to my sister, Joan Gallaher, and to my cousin, Esmee (Townley) Mansell, who have both provided data for my entries; to my wife, Marion, who never faltered with help, encouragement, and patience; to Suzanne Bastedo for her enthusiasm and editorial expertise; and to Diana Douglas and the people connected with Peanut Butter Publishing. Thank you all.

For my efforts on this manuscript I feel the posthumous approbation of my mother, Gertie, and her sisters, and of Wallace's beloved Cecie. If you, the dispassionate reader, discover something worthwhile in the pages, I will realize a deep pleasure.

∽

Introduction

~

Wallace Chambers was born in Winnipeg, Manitoba, in 1886, two years after the Canadian Pacific Railway (C.P.R.) disgorged the first immigrants to settle in the future city of Vancouver. His parents, Samuel and Lizzie Chambers (née Elizabeth Watts), had said goodbye to their parents in Woodstock, Upper Canada, and settled in Manitoba as part of the migration of hopeful young Canadians taking advantage of what the railway had opened up. Wallace and his five sisters were all born in Manitoba; Wallace was the fourth child.

Three years before Wallace was born, Samuel purchased ten acres in the County of Shoal Lake at Birtle, Manitoba. But rumours of greater opportunities further west put the family on the train to the promising rich coal deposits of the Crowsnest Pass. They settled in Blairmore, Alberta. Samuel and a partner opened three hardware stores — one in Blairmore, one in nearby Coleman, and another two miles east, in Frank. Life proceeded uneventfully for the Chambers family until June 13, 1902, when Lizzie, at age fifty-three, had a fatal stroke. At that time, Wallace was sixteen, Susan, thirteen, and Gertie, just eleven. Providentially, a team of three well-balanced older

Maude, Mary and Edith Chambers, circa 1900

sisters — Maude, Edith, and Mary — took on the mothering role for the younger ones.

The next year, on April 29, 1903, another catastrophe struck in the form of the massive Frank Slide. Ninety million tons of Turtle Mountain buried much of Frank and destroyed Samuel's ability to see his way out of debt. In

Sign photographed at the site of the Frank Slide, Alberta.
(For more information, see *The Frank Slide* by J. William Kerr, 1990,
Barker Publishing Co., Box 16, Site 8, R.R. 1, Pridis, Alberta T0L 1W0)

1906, he and his children boarded a C.P.R. train heading for the promise of a better life in the growing city of Vancouver. Exactly when Samuel died, or how, was an unmentionable topic in the family.

This book has been organized with one goal uppermost: to retain the freshness of Wallace's words by giving only enough background commentary to provide context. As much as possible, therefore, I have reproduced Wallace's diary entries as he wrote them, including using his spelling and punctuation. The book begins with Wallace's letters from the trenches in 1915. The succeeding chapters start with the 1907 diary entries of Wallace, who was then living with his sisters in Vancouver. These diary entries are organized according to themes which were important to Wallace in a particular year — for instance, social, cultural, and outdoor activities; church; work; real estate investments; military activities, and Cecie, the woman who would eventually become his wife. Since Wallace's diary ends on December 31, 1913, the final chapter sheds some light on Wallace's life from then to his first letter from the front in 1915. The book closes with a postscript about Wallace and Cecie.

~

Chapter 1

~

1915

"I'm Proud To Be a Canadian"

Women all, hear the call,
The pitiless call of WAR.
Look your last on your dearest ones,
Brothers and husbands, fathers and sons.
Swift they go to the ravenous guns,
The gluttonous guns of WAR.

— Robert Service, "The Call"[1]

When Britain declared war against Germany on August 4, 1914, Canada was lockstep with the Mother Country in its determination to halt the threat of German aggression. Amongst the earliest recruits in Vancouver was Wallace Chambers, who had been sworn in with Vancouver's 72nd Regiment of the Canadian Scottish on December 17, 1910. When war was declared, this regiment united with three other Canadian Highlander regiments — 50th Gordon Highlanders (Victoria); 79th Cameron Highlanders (Winnipeg); 91st Canadian Highlanders (Hamilton) — to form the 16th Battalion (The Canadian Scottish). On

September 30, 1914, having mustered at Valcartier,
Quebec, they set sail on SS *Andania*, for Plymouth,
England, thence to Salisbury Plains where they would
train over the winter. In February, the main body of the
16th Battalion sailed for France, and were soon in mortal
combat with the enemy, in the region of Ypres.

Wallace was amongst a group of reinforcements to the
battle-weary and decimated regiment on April 27, 1915.
On the night of April 22, the battalion had suffered heavy
casualties while counter-attacking a German offensive in
the second battle of Ypres. Amongst the wounded was
their machine gun officer, Lieut. Reginald Tupper. Wallace
would be his replacement.

Wallace's letters from the front were characteristic of
him. In the midst of shelling and death, he still noticed
the colour of the sky and the beauty of the countryside
around him. Gertie, Sue, Edith, and Maude were Wallace's
sisters; Cecie his wife; Dr. Gillies[2] was another
Vancouverite; Capt. Kemp was Wallace's great friend with
whom he shared billets. "Billets" referred to the fact that
when not at the front, the soldiers stayed with local
families.

～

May 1st, 1915
Belgium

Dearest Maude,

*We are in trenches near Ypres — lovely sunny
weather. The birds are singing in the intervals between
bombardments and it is almost possible to forget for
awhile that we are in the thick of a terrible battle. The
French attacked last night and captured some trenches
and prisoners. I saw the prisoners — but the price of*

victory is awful. I've just come over from the dressing station — poor beggars dreadfully mutilated. The cheerfulness of our chaps is remarkable. Shelling has commenced again. I'll have to sit tight in the dugout. We are due for a rest now soon. When we will get into billets I'll write a long letter.

Love to all, Wallace.

~

16th Battalion, 3rd Brigade,
The Canadian Scottish, C.E.F. France
May 4th, 1915

Dear Maude,

When we reached Boulogne we immediately joined the Regiment who were just behind the trenches in bivouac and that same night were ordered into the trenches again, so it wasn't very long getting into the thick of it, and by Jove, war is <u>horrible</u>. No one can understand by reading the papers what it is like. The shells kept dropping and bursting all around us and those that were going beyond us into Ypres gave an angry whistle or screech as they passed. Last Sunday night one dropped on our Machine Gun dugout and killed four men. I am officer of the Machine Gun Battery now. I took the course at Hythe and now have taken Reggie Tupper's place.

I have a saddle horse and the position is a nice one as well as being important. I am on the Regimental Staff in this capacity, so mess with the Colonel, Major Leckie, W.F. Kemp, Adjutant, Dr. Gillies, and Capt. Markham, the signalling officer.

You pretty nearly lost your brother the other day. The Colonel sent me on a message and sent his servant with me (we never go about singly). Well, just as a French soldier came along, I heard a terrific bang. I was thrown several feet in the air and stunned, and my thoughts were: well, the Germans have got me. However, I was surprised when I sat up and looked around to find I wasn't hurt, only a little cut on my finger and a hole in my coat. The shell had made a huge hole in the ground not six feet in front of me. The servant was badly wounded and the poor Frenchman killed. It was an awful shock you may imagine. Then I ran back and got a stretcher and two men, and had the servant carried in, and all the time those darn shells were banging all around.

We have been withdrawn from the trenches now and are camped beyond the range of guns, thank the Lord.

General Sir Horace Dorien-Smith called on us yesterday and we were introduced to him. He spoke very feelingly of the Canadians, of their bravery, and of the gallantry of our fellows who have lost their lives. While he was speaking, I could not keep the tears back to save my life. He thanked Col. Leckie and all of us for our behaviour under heavy fire. He was proud of the Canadian Scottish and said the Canadians were recognized by the War Office to be second to none, and had proved it.

Later — I have just come in from a fine ride on my horse which is a beauty. This country is delightful, the fruit trees are all in blossom — nice farm houses. I had supper at one last night. It was great fun. Their staple food is brown bread and coffee. The peasants seem to eat nothing else. I made out that I wanted two boiled eggs, which were fresh and cooked to a nicety, and all the time the people were bowing and scraping and gave me a towel for a serviette. The peasants treat British officers like Lords.

We shall be here for a week's rest, then into the trenches again. I must not say anything about our movements but no doubt we are going to see all the fighting we want. You will have seen the casualties reported ere this. I'll have my work cut out for me now, getting my new men trained in the Machine Gun work.

Give my love to Edith, Sue, Gertie and lots to you, my dear sister.

Wallace.

~

The following were excerpted from Wallace's letters to Cecie. As Cecie wrote to Maude on Thursday, May 6, 1915: "Two letters from Wallace last night so I will copy portions of them for you."

~

1st May: Isn't this a perfectly lovely morning. The sun is so warm and the birds cheer us with their sweet notes when we have a few moments cessation from the awful noise of the guns. Your two sweet letters came up to me last night. Jove, I do love your letters more than ever, Sweetheart. Our chaplain is splendid bringing the mail every day, usually under heavy fire.

Kemp is now Adjutant and I am sitting beside him in the trench now. He asked kindly after you and wished to be remembered to you, dear. They all did, in fact. I am on the regimental staff now. You know this honour accompanies the position of Machine Gun Officer so the Colonel, adjutant, doctor, signalling officer and myself mess together. I haven't had my clothes off since I left England and we don't know when we will have the opportunity. No sleep, either, to speak of, just an hour or so now and then.

There are a lot of French wounded on stretchers just behind our trenches and just now a German shell broke right over them probably pulling most of them out of their misery. Jove, Cecie, you have no idea of the <u>awfulness</u> of this war. No one could realize unless they were right here on the ground. The cheerfulness of our chaps is remarkable. Jove, they are behaving splendidly.

Kemp has just had word that we are to be relieved in a day or so — then we will go back out of range for awhile and get rested and cleaned up and reorganized. There is a sergeant just leaving for the base P.O. so will have to close.

May 3rd/15: The battle is still going on and we are occupying the same trenches which are in the rear of the actual firing line which is about 300 yards in front of us. At present the French are up in them and we are acting as a reserve for them in case they are driven back. They are very plucky indeed and their stretcher bearers are very brave, walking right up to the firing line, picking up the wounded and bringing them to the field hospital, apparently oblivious to the bullets whizzing about. It really is a marvel that more of them are not hit. We have improved our trenches and now feel quite safe in them during a bombardment. This morning we had it hot and heavy — the big high explosive shells (60 pounds) fairly rained in on us but only one did any damage — killed one chap outright and badly mangled another (both Canadian Officers of the Montreal Battery). I'm very thankful, dear, that my nerves are good and that I'm naturally cool-headed —

*one certainly needs to be amongst the sights and noise.
The Yser canal is very much like the one at Sandgate,
lovely tall trees on either side, but the surroundings, how
different!! The Germans are after us again, but we will
sit in here laughing at them.*

Au revoir. Wallace.

~

France, Sunday, 9th May, 1915

Dear Maude,

*We are still in billets and expect to be for a day or so
yet. It is very much more pleasant than in the trenches,
I can tell you. I have a splendid horse of my own now
and went for a glorious ride today.*

*General Alderson inspected us today and said lots of
nice things about the good work of the "Canadian
Scottish".*

*We have just come in from Divine Service. It was held
in a barnyard — pigs running about, etc., but a more
devout congregation I never saw. We hadn't any hymn
books but sang the well-known ones — "Jesus Lover of
My Soul", "Abide With Me", and "Holy, Holy, Holy". The
chaplain gave us a very good address. I wish I could
have had a snapshot of it to send to you.*

*I have another officer in the Machine Gun Battery
now to assist me and if God spares me I don't think it
will be long before your humble servant will be a
captain. That will be nice, eh, dear?*

*I am kept so busy that I've hardly time to write to
anyone. I write a note to Cecie every day. She is a
darling and writes me lovely letters every day.*

Isn't it awful that the Germans have sunk the Lusitania? I'm glad Harold and Ian have joined, altho' it will be hard on Aunt Rose and Uncle George.

Lots of love to Gertie, Sue, Edith and to yourself from your affectionate brother, Wallace

P.S. France is a beautiful country in the springtime especially. The big guns have been booming all day.

～

In the latter part of May 1915, the 16th Battalion made themselves famous in the Battle of Festubert-Givenchy. They succeeded in routing the enemy from an orchard, thereafter called "The Canadian Orchard." Wallace spoke of his machine guns having been placed in an advanced position, aiding the attackers. The attack was witnessed by a Coldstreamer (British) who was quoted in *The History of the 16th Battalion*: "The Canadians went into the attack just as if they were drilling in Hyde Park. Each man at about two paces interval going at a walking pace with the enemy's machine guns and rifle fire on a wide front turned on them. It gives us better courage to know we have such men to rely on" (1932: p. 79).

～

May 24th, 1915

Dear Maude,

You will have heard about our charge on the evening of the 20th when we captured a position that several British regiments failed to do previously. We got a

German Machine Gun as well. The night before the attack I placed two of my guns 200 yards in advance of our trenches and concealed them behind a hedge. When the battalion attacked, these two guns played on the Germans at close range, completely surprising them. It was ticklish work that night — placing those guns out there, so close to the Germans. They fired at us but none of us were hit, but the next night the German artillery spotted these two guns and dropped a shell on them, killing two of my men, and wounding nine. Sgt. Kindred was one of the wounded. I think Sue knows him. The Battalion lost 280 wounded.

Later: I have ridden in to Bethune, a town you have probably read about. It's splendid having a horse as I can see so much more of the country.

We go back to the trenches tomorrow night. I'm sending some men up tonight to get the German Machine Gun we captured. I've only got a minute to spare.

Please give my love to Edith, Arthur, Phyllis when you write, and Gertie and Sue and the Gibsons.

Much love to you, dear Maude,
Your affectionate brother, Wallace

∼

Cecie copied out more excerpts from Wallace's letters to her, and sent them to Maude. Where Wallace asked for a cake with raisins in it, Cecie added a note of her own: "Doesn't this sound natural? The dear boy." The part about what Colonel Leckie said was likely deleted by a censor, who checked all outgoing letters from military personnel.

∼

May 15th/15: This has been another lovely day. This afternoon at four I went for a ride to Caronne Sur La Lys not very far from Lille. The country is beautiful. We have just finished dinner now and as we didn't sleep much last night, I'm going to turn in soon. Don't bother sending any more tobacco as I haven't nearly finished the last yet, and we have it issued to us, also cigs. for those who smoke them. There isn't really anything I need just now, dear, but for my birthday, a cake with raisins in it would be very nice. Then I'd take it to mess and tell them my wife made it, and share it with them, but don't go to the bother of icing it, just plain cake that you made with your own dear hands and of course, a note in with it. I love your letters more than anything else you can send. Au revoir. W.

May 21st/15: We have just returned from the front line of trenches and are now in the reserve line. We were in the La Bassee fight and our battalion attacked last night. You will see an account of it in the papers and the casualty list later on. I came through without injury but you must excuse this note my darling, as my nerves are all on edge. Dick Wallis, Colquhoun, Kemp and I have just been talking about the affair last night. It was a difficult point to hold on to. Col. Leckie says ———— .

May 25, 1915: France, The Canadian Scottish C.E.F. Another ripping day and we are now standing ready to go back to the firing line and have another go at the Allemands. Dick Wallis and I had a glorious swim in the Canal de la Basses. I received the cake of soap you sent out, dearest. Thank you very much. We expected to move again tonight but I think it will not be until tomorrow now. I was talking to Crowdy just now and we congratulated each other on coming out of that affair without being wounded. Did I tell you that we captured a German machine gun? I am the only Machine Gunner left in our Brigade. I was at the Brigade Head Quarters this A.M. drilling the Batteries of the 13th, 14th and 15th Batteries.

Just now we were watching the Germans shooting at a French observation balloon near here. The little puffs of smoke look so pretty in the blue sky. You wouldn't suspect how vicious they are really. However all the shells are falling far short so no harm is being done.

I am sitting here by an open window looking across beautiful green fields dotted with trees at another beautiful sunset. The whole scene is so peaceful and lovely. As I look out the window one of our aeroplanes came over close to us and dropped a message. They do splendid work. Au revoir, Wallace.

May 26, 1915: Bethune, France. I brought my men in to Bethune for baths and Duncan and I have just finished lunch at the Café Paun D'Hor. This is quite a large town and the nicest I have seen so far. We are to be back to the firing line tonight, which is not a pleasant prospect, but still it is our duty, so we'll stay with it. The Battalion paraded this A.M., Col. Leckie telling us a lot of nice things about our work. Two of our Sergeants won the Distinguished Conduct Medal. This is a delightfully warm day.

Au revoir. Wallace.

~

Wallace was so immersed in the war that in the following excerpt from a letter to Cecie, he said that he would be turning thirty when in fact he would only be turning twenty-nine.

~

France, 29th of May, 1915: An orderly has just come over and told me that several of our chaps were wounded by those shells that dropped a while ago. I must go and see them. Goodbye for a few minutes.

Oh darling, those d———— shells struck eleven of our chaps wounding some of them very badly. It makes my blood boil. Germany will pay dearly for it all, Cecie dear. Some of those wounded are Dick Wallis' men.

Tomorrow will be my birthday. By Jingo, I'll be 30! I am writing this in the Orderly Room. The Colonel is here, and Major Rae, Capt. Kemp, and Markham. Kemp is a fine chap. We are bunking together. I have to go and do some work now dear. I hope everything is well with you. Etc. Etc.

Your affectionate husband, Wallace.

~

On June 5, Wallace began a journal describing a week in the trenches. The battalion was in the Givenchy front, in the trench system east of Givenchy-lez-la-Bassee. This period turned out to be a relatively uneventful time.

A Week In The Trenches
June 5, 1915

Obleugem, France: Orders to proceed to trenches at Givenchy with my men and four machine guns. Left 10 P.M. Marched through Bethune and reached a point on the La Basse Canal (at rear of trenches) at 1 A.M. The 7th Battalion had a guide here who directed us to the firing line, about a mile in front. Whilst going up we were sniped at by the Germans but we reached our destination without casualties — a good part of the way we were in communication trenches.

We got the guns set up by 3 A.M. This portion of the trench is called Oxford St., and all the trenches are called London street names, viz. Regent St., Piccadilly, Curzon St., etc. I have a good dugout in Bond St. with a sign over the doorway "Romano's".

At the front (Wallace on the left). France, 1915

June 6, 1915

5:00 A.M. No shelling. I turned in and had three hours sleep. My batman awakened me for breakfast. A few shells knocking about. One just hit a corporal of the 15th Battalion which is in reserve just behind us. The poor chap died instantly.

Noon. Very hot. The dugout is cool, though.

8:30 P.M. Went to headquarters in rear to see adjutant. On the way back inspected the Mach. gun posts of the 15th Battalion. Up all night visiting my guns which are in different parts of the line. One gun is placed in a spot not more than 50 yards from the enemy trench.

We all stand to arms an hour before dawn, the men with bayonets fixed in anticipation of a German attack, although we know they don't like attacking us. Fairly quiet night.

June 7th, 1915

5:00 A.M. Turned in and slept until 9:00 A.M. Left instructions with sentry to awaken me in case of an alarm.

10 A.M. Bristol returned with a huge bunch of lovely red roses. He gathered them in a garden in the rear of our lines. They adorn our dugout now. I'd love to send them to Cecie.

2 P.M. Standing to with respirators adjusted as the wind is favourable for use of gas by the enemy.

3 P.M. No gas in sight yet. The mail has just been brought up to us. I got a sweet letter from Cecie, and one from Maude. Jove, we appreciate getting letters, and Cecie sends such cheering ones. Spent the afternoon walking about the trenches and dropping in and chatting with the different officers. We hear heavy

Above: Wallace (left) and fellow officer.
Below: Wallace in trench. France, 1915

Wallace at "Oxford St." trench. France, 1915

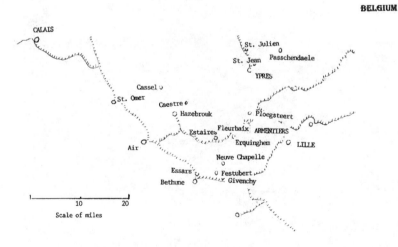

Map of the front and surrounding area. France, 1915.
Based on information from *History of the 16th Battalion (The Canadian
Scottish): Canadian Expeditionary Force in the Great War, 1914–1919,*
by H.M. Urquart, The MacMillan Company of Canada, Limited,
St. Martin's House, 1932

16

cannonading over to our right. In Jones' dugout we had red wine and biscuits.

6:30 P.M. Just finished tea. It's cooler now. Very hot this afternoon. The German snipers are busy all the time. I was looking over the parapet just now using my periscope. I hadn't held it long before a bullet hit the sandbag beside me. We don't stay above the parapet very long. Staying awake night and day practically doesn't worry us. Of course it begins to tell on one after four or five days.

June 8th, 1915

3:30 A.M. Trench mortars were firing on our left at 1:30 A.M. German snipers busy all night. It is quite light now. Lovely morning. The birds are twittering sweetly.

4:00 A.M. German guns shelling in the vicinity of our Reserve trenches.

4:20 A.M. Captain Wood, Powis, Bristol, and I have a cup of tea in my dugout. I'm going to turn in for a couple of hour's sleep, as there isn't anything exciting going on — just a few shells, and the usual sniping.

Awakened at 8 A.M. The roses are still fresh. It was quiet all morning until 11 A.M. when our guns opened on the German trenches. I went up into an old house and observed the fire. We put many shrapnel into their trench. A letter from Cecie, and one from Sue came up to me this morning.

2:30 P.M. Thunder and a little rain about noon. Cloudy now. Shells are whizzing about like the deuce.

5 P.M. I've just returned from visiting Capt. Wood in his dugout. I went over as he was all alone in his dugout and it's not pleasant to be absolutely alone during a bombardment.

June 9th, 1915

Up all night. The usual sniping going on. I turned in at 4 A.M. and slept until 9 A.M. Our artillery bombarded their trenches all day. Cut up their barb wire entanglements pretty badly.

7 P.M. Corporal Thompson went out in front of our line reconnoitring and got within 20 yards of their trench without being seen. There is a field of rye between our trenches about three feet high.

8:30 P.M. Germans threw over three bombs, but did no damage.

9:30 P.M. Sentry reports he heard someone moving about in front. I put up two flares from my Verey pistol but none of the enemy visible.

11:30 P.M. Sniping on both sides.

June 10th, 1915

The sniping developed into heavy rifle fire. I fired a few rounds with one of my machine guns. The ration party has just come in with food and mail. There were three letters from Cecie, enclosing one from Maude and Sue. Cecie writes me lovely letters. Also there was a P.C. for me from Evelyn and Nona. Cecie says her father has just returned from South America. I'm glad he returned safely. The rifle fire has subsided for a while.

8 A.M. Started to rain a little.

3 P.M. until 5 P.M. Raining heavily. The trenches are fearfully muddy. Our artillery firing all day.

9 P.M. Started sniping again, which kept up all night, at times developing into a fusillade. The Germans threw several grenades at us. Only one did any damage —knocked a hole in our trench, but we soon repaired it. It is rumoured that we are to attack tomorrow night.

June 11th, 1915

*6 P.M. Order has just come to move out tonight.
Hoorah! The Highland Light Infantry relieved us at 7 P.M.
but we didn't leave until dark. Arrived at our billets at
Essars near Bethune, 3 A.M.*

~

As a letter to his uncle in Vancouver showed, Wallace
remained strongly convinced of the correctness of his
soldierly duties despite his experiences at the front —
so much so that he was glad that his cousins, Harold and
Ian, had enlisted. The "foul means" to which Wallace
referred was the employment of asphyxiating gas by the
Germans. "E.C. & E." referred to Evans, Coleman & Evans,
Wallace's employers in Vancouver.

~

*Canadian Scottish, France
16th June, 1915*

My dear Uncle George,

*I was delighted to get your letter today. Yes, I agree
with you in your expression of disgust in the way the
Germans are resorting to every foul means to bring
about England's downfall. However, we'll never give up
until we've crushed her — although the toll has been
awful, and will be more awful before it's finished.*

*There is a big battle on now — it started last night
and the 1st Brigade of the Canadians are in it. There
has been a heavy cannonading going on and I hear
from the wounded going past here that our casualties*

have been heavy — but the Germans heavier still. Our Brigade (the 3rd) is ordered up and we are standing to, now ready to move off.

I passed my exams in England as Machine Gun Officer and am now in charge of four guns. I have a fine horse to ride, which is very nice, especially when we are in billets for a few days. I usually go for a ride every day, and in this way see a good deal of the country which is looking beautiful just now.

I'm glad Harold and Ian have enlisted. I think it's the duty of every able-bodied young man to help bring about the downfall of that monster, "Kaiser Bill". One of our ammunition wagons has stenciled on the back "Kultur Kure".

I am feeling awfully fit, and if it were not for the hideous side of war, I would enjoy the excitement of it — but some of my best pals have been killed which brings home to one more than anything else the awfulness of this struggle. It would do your heart good to see the way our chaps go forward when the order to charge is given. By Jove! I'm proud to be a Canadian.

I am looking forward to the time when this thing is over, when my wife and I will see you all in Vancouver. Cecie writes the most cheering letters. I am indeed a lucky boy to have such a fine girl as my wife.

E.C. & E. are treating me well, aren't they? Business with you must be quiet, I suppose.

Remember me to Dr. Mackay when you see him. With much love to dear Aunt Rose, and Jessie & Agnes.

Ever your affectionate nephew, Wallace.

～

Wallace and his horse. France, June 1915

Contrary to Wallace's reassurances to his sisters, machine gunners were at great risk since they had to leave the protection of the trench to set up their emplacements. Wallace received a fatal wound on July 6, 1915.

Cecie received the following two letters telling her about his death.

~

France, 6 July, 1915

Dear Mrs. Chambers,

I am very sorry to tell you that your husband died this morning of wounds received at midnight last night. It has been a great shock to us all and we offer you our sincere sympathy. He died a true soldier's death, and was most plucky when wounded. I will tell you about it.

His men were making emplacements for the guns. He came around to see how one emplacement was getting on and asked the men if it were not too new-looking in front, so he and Cpl. Thomas went outside the parapet to look at it. This was about midnight. There was a little moonlight at the time. They lay down for a few minutes then stood up and bent down to examine the loop-hole. Just then he cried, "I'm hit," and groaned a bit. Thomas asked him to bear it for a minute, and not groan as the Germans might hear it; after that he did not make a noise. Then Thomas called through the loop-hole for the stretcher-bearers. Private McFarlane and two bearers came out and got him over. He thanked them for the trouble he was giving them. He also said, "I'm sorry that I could not have a chance to get at them with the guns," and wished the boys good luck before he was carried out to the Norfolks Dressing Station. Sgt. Donald went down with him. He asked them to be sure to give his field glasses &c to Capt. Forgie for safety as they were a present from you. His wound, which was in the thigh, was re-dressed there. Sgt. Donald left him there and his last instructions to Donald were to be sure that the emplacement was finished. He was then taken to #38 Field Ambulance and must have lost consciousness on the way. The doctor says he must have recovered consciousness for a few seconds an hour after his arrival and said, "I hope you don't think I am fussing too much." He evidently had no idea he was seriously wounded.

He died at 4:30 A.M. As I could not possibly leave the Battalion, I asked Hon. Capt. Heakes to look after the funeral. He was laid in the British Military Cemetery at Armentiers at 2:30 P.M. The service was read by Rev. Alfred T. Morgan of the 38th Field Ambulance. There was a guard of honour of fifty men. All his effects have been collected, and will be sent to you.

I thought it best to tell you everything. It is very hard to express my thoughts but I hope you will find great consolation in the fact that your husband played the game throughout and died a true soldier's death.

Please let me know if there is anything I can possibly do for you.

Yours very sincerely,
Walter P. Kemp

Belgium, July 7, 1915

To Mrs. S.W.G. Chambers,
London, England

Dear Mrs. Chambers,

In sending under separate cover a parcel of personal belongings, may I be permitted to add my assurance to that of fellow officers who have already written to you, of the very keen sorrow we all feel at the loss of one so much beloved among us and so highly regarded by all who knew him.

Knowing that even the slightest details will be of value to you, I send the following:

Mr. Chambers was taken to 38th Field Ambulance Hospital where everything possible was done to nurse the spark of life which remained after his arrival there, Lieut. Milne M.D. being the officer in charge of the case.

The officer Commanding the hospital ordered out a Guard of Honour of fifty men for the funeral which took place at 2:30 P.M. July 6th from the hospital to the British Cemetery on the Erquinham Road, near Ecole National, Armentiers. The service was conducted by Rev. Alfred T. Morgan, the chaplain attached to the 38th Field Ambulance.

Capt. S.V. Heakes, Paymaster of the 16th Battalion, who was the only officer present (the regiment being in the trenches), asks me to assure you that everything that could possibly be done was done both in the hospital and in connection with the funeral, which was carried out with full military honours, the grave being properly marked.

I enclose a list given me by Capt. Heakes of articles in Mr. Chamber's possession at the time of his injury. I take it for granted that you will find all the smaller articles enclosed in the handkerchief which I have forwarded just as received from him. The Wolseley sleeping bag and kit will go forward to you tomorrow but will necessarily take some time in transport.

I enclose also a letter which arrived after Mr. Chambers had gone to the trenches on July 5th and was not delivered to him, also a snap shot which may be of some interest to you.

Again assuring you of the sincere sympathy of myself and fellow officers and of my readiness to render you any service within my power, I remain,

Respectfully yours,
Wallace Forgie, Capt.

~

Wallace Chambers' grave. July 7, 1915

Notes

1. Robert Service, "The Call." Written in France, August 1, 1914 (from *Rhythmes of a Red Cross Man*, published by William Briggs in Toronto, 1916). Also see *More Selected Verse of Robert Service*, reprinted in 1976 (River City Press, P.O. Box 1200, Mattituck, New York 11952).

2. Dr. Gillies refers to George Ernest Gillies, who enlisted with the 16th Battalion on September 22, 1914, served with the Canadian Army Medical Corps until September 2, 1915, thence to Salonika (now Thessalonica), Greece.

Chapter 2

~

1907

"Had a Lovely Time"

In 1906, after the Chambers family moved to Vancouver, an uncle, George Gibson, the general manager of the Pacific Coast Lumber Company, hired Wallace as book-keeper. Wallace and his five sisters rented a house at 1155 Georgia Street,[1] just five blocks from Wallace's work at 1605 Georgia. Susan (also called Sue, Suse, or Susie) was eighteen, and closest in age to Wallace. The other sisters living with Wallace included Gertie, sixteen; Maude, thirty-four; and Mary, thirty-two. Gertie was still at school, and Maude worked as a nurse. Mary may have helped keep house for the others. Edith, another older sister, lived elsewhere in Vancouver. She was married to Arthur Blanchet, who had been an accountant for the family business in Blairmore.

Twenty-year-old Wallace started keeping a diary in 1907. He began in a rather desultory way. Days, some-times weeks, passed without an entry. In later years, he became more committed. His recorded interests in 1907 generally revolved around social, outdoor, and cultural activities. As far as his diary was concerned, Cecie, the woman he would one day marry, was still a minor theme.

Social Activities

In 1907, Wallace wrote not about his work or any aspirations he might have had for a career, but about his friends and the activities he enjoyed with them.

~

At dance at Grangers. Jan. 25, 1907

Connie G, Susie and I. Skating on Trout Lake.
Jan. 28/07

Evening skating on Trout Lake. Connie G., Suse and
Futcher. Saturday, Feb. 2/07

Ladies Hockey Club Ball. Went with Susie, Connie
Granger, and Emilia Fernau. Had a lovely time.
Feb. 1/07

At Miss Holmes' dance, Pender Hall. Very good time.
Fri. Feb. 15th/07

Went yachting on the Granger's yacht "Alisa". Sailed
to Roche Point, had tea and came back under power.
Connie, Ella, Gertie, Susy, Lily Armstrong, Francis
Anderson, Boake, McCrimmon, Mr. Granger & Mr.
Brydon-Jack, & Robby. Very jolly time. Sat. afternoon,
Sept. 7/07

~

Wallace and his sister, Sue, made friends their own age quickly in Vancouver. Many of their friends were mutual, and they often shared social outings. Sue and her friends were Wallace's companions for dances and other outings such as skating at Trout Lake. Connie Granger, a friend Wallace mentioned often in 1907, was a school teacher at Strathcona School and lived at her family's home.[2]

The young people were socially active on week nights as well as on weekends. They often congregated in private homes for their parties. The Granger house, for instance, was the site of many dances and social activities. Sometimes a family hosted a private dance at a local hall, such as the "Miss Holmes dance" Wallace mentioned in February. And joining the Rowing Club in May reaped social benefits for Wallace in December.

~

Joined the Van. Rowing Club. May 1/07

Had our first club dance in St. Paul's Hall. Jolly good time. About 34 were there. Miss Hornby, Gradwell, Leighton, Davis, Chambers, Brenton, Henshaw, Clyne, Jenkinson, Allen. Mrs. Blanchet, Thompson, Lindsay. Mr. Anderson, Colquhoun, Large, Shannon, Smythe, Grundy, Sweeny, Harvey, Dickey, Allen, Lindsay, Chambers, Blanchet, and others.
Mon. Dec. 9/07

~

Outdoors

Wallace obviously enjoyed being in the outdoors. After purchasing a canoe in January, he did not waste much time putting it to use. Throughout the year, he also went hiking and camping, often with his brother-in-law, Arthur, who was his companion for many outdoor and cultural events.

~

Bought canoe from Wadds; pd him $25.00.
Jan. 15/07

Went canoeing yesterday with Connie Granger and
Suse. Sunday, Feb. 17th/07

Beautiful day. Arthur and I went for a paddle in the
canoe to Deep Cove & Bedwell Bay. Met the Granger's
party on their yacht — had lunch with them. When
we were coming home Susie and Syd Dyke upset out
of a canoe. No harm except a drenching. Further
down near the Narrows, N. Granger & Simpson
upset. We left Belcarra at 6:30 and arrived home at
8:45. Tide was with us. Very tired. May 24/07

Very warm. Arthur and I went for a walk up the
Lynn Valley, walked about twenty miles, came back
by the Seymour Creek valley. Sun. June 2nd/07

~

In the following entry about camping, "G.F.G. and the boys" referred to Wallace's uncle (and boss) George Gibson, and his two sons, Harold and Ian. After the tiring weekend and a long paddle home before going to work on Monday, Wallace may have preferred to go to bed early Monday night. His notes gave no hint of such a preference, however, as he identified the guests who dropped in that evening. Strangely, he included Gertie, who was part of his own household, as part of the group "coming up," a term that he used as in "coming up to visit." Perhaps Gertie had been returning from a visit with Mrs. Gigot?

~

Arthur & I, G.F.G. and the boys camping to Bedwell Bay. Went up on Sat. P.M. came back early Monday A.M., up at 4:00 A.M. had swim and breakfast, left camp at 5:30 reached Vancouver at 8:00. Paddled about 15 miles. Pretty tired all day. In the evening Mrs. Gigot and Gertie came up, also Futcher and Connie Granger. Went to bed at 12:30. July 20th/07

~

Two more outdoor activities merited mention in Wallace's diary this year. The first was a canoe trip starting from Sydney on Vancouver Island.[3] The second was a fifty-mile paddle.

~

In the morning met Edith and Arthur at Victoria, went straightaway to Sydney. Splendid grub. Saturday got our canoe from Vancouver and started out on a paddle, camped in Deep Cove Sat. night. Sunday crossed Saanich Inlet. Saw several whales. Had lunch in Cowichan Bay, thence to Genoa Bay & Maple Bay to Crofton, came back, camped in a delightful spot just inside Burgoyne Bay on Salt Spring Island. Just as we were leaving Burgoyne Bay a big wave struck us and filled the canoe nearly half full, fortunately we were near the shore so just unloaded the things and dried them, paddled across Satellite Channel by moonlight which was glorious. Tuesday night camped in Deep Cove and paddled back to Sydney, arriving in the evening of Wednesday. Aug. 10/07

Went up to Indian River with Arthur and came back as far as Coon Isle and camped, Monday being Labour Day. Got 4 grouse. Arrived home about 4:00 P.M. Monday — 50 mile paddle. Sept. 1/07

~

Cultural Activities
This year, Wallace began to indulge his developing passion for cultural events.

~

Went to see Olga Nethersole play "The Second Mrs. Tanqueray". Arthur came with me. Jan. 30/07

Arthur and I went to see "She Stoops to Conquer". Feb. 5/07

Went to "Madam Butterfly" — Savage's Grand Opera Co. Very good but pathetic. Mar. 5/07

Went to see Nat Goodwin on Saturday. Played the Gilded Fool. Edna Goodrich is awfully pretty. Apr. 30/07

Took Connie G. to see "Prince of Pilson" which was good. Oct. 17/07

Maude and I went to hear Calvé. By Jove, it was a treat. Dec. 2/07

~

Church
Wallace was a regular at St. John's Presbyterian[4] Church, 1401 Comox Street, which he attended alone or with others.

~

Walked around Stanley Park with Arthur. Church in the evening. Sunday Feb. 3rd/07

Mary and I went to St. John's Church. Sun Feb. 10th/07

Went to church twice. Miss La Londe sang solo St. John's Church. Sunday Feb. 17th/07

~

Cecie
Wallace first met Cecilia (Cecie) Fernau in Blairmore. Her father was a mining engineer who travelled extensively. In 1905, he had brought his family to Blairmore on business for a few months, then returned to their home in London, England. Although Wallace and Cecie were already corresponding,[5] Wallace did no more than note Cecie's nineteenth birthday in his 1907 diary.

~

Cecilia's birthday 19 years today. Feb. 22/07

~

Notes

1. The following were recorded to be the heads of households on the same side of the block: 1155 Georgia, Wallace Chambers; 1159 Georgia, Annex Glencoe Lodge; 1163 Georgia, Jonathon Rogers; 1167 Georgia, George Phipps; 1175 Georgia, Alexander Munro, M.D.

2. The Granger home was at 1640 Harwood Avenue. Connie's father was R.T.F. Granger, Chief Clerk of the Land Registry Office.

3. The Deep Cove mentioned is the one on Vancouver Island, not the one on British Columbia's mainland.

4. St. John's eventually became a United Church.

5. Wallace made no mention of his early correspondence with Cecie until his 1912 diary, where he said that he was rereading 1905 and 1906 letters he had received from her.

Chapter 3

~

1909

"Played Bridge at Hornby's"

What happened to 1908? What happened *in* 1908? With a one-year gap, Wallace enigmatically continued his diary in the same journal, with 1909 following 1907 in logical sequence! There was a further gap of three and one-half months, from April 24 to August 10, when Wallace misplaced his journal. Wallace's entries this year reflected his burgeoning social and cultural interests.

Work

The 1909 diary began with Wallace apparently nonchalant about losing his position at the Pacific Coast Lumber Mills when the company folded. Though jobs were scarce, and times hard, he soon landed a bookkeeping job paying $80 per month with the firm, Evans, Coleman & Evans.[1] This was a robust and multifaceted company which acted as suppliers for builders and industries such as canneries and railways; as agents and brokers for steamships such as the Pacific Mail Steamship Company, the Terminal Steamship Company, the SS *Brittania,* the SS *Defiance,* and the SS *Belcarra;* and as agents for fire and marine insurance. As in 1907, Wallace's diary paid scant attention to work matters, and focused more on his social, cultural, and outdoor calendars, which were busy indeed.

~

Left the Pc. Coast Lbr. Mills where I held the post of Cashier & Book-keeper for 2 years & 10 months. Jan. 31/09

Spent the last ten days in looking for a position. Saw Mr. P.W. Evans today, of Evans Coleman & Evans — may get on with them. Feb. 12/09

Hired with Evans Coleman & Evans at $80.00 per mo., start on Monday Feb. 15. Feb. 13/09

~

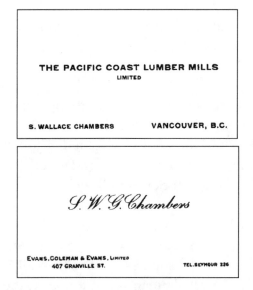

Wallace's business cards at Pacific Coast Lumber
and at Evans, Coleman & Evans

Evans, Coleman & Evans advertisement, 1908

Social Activities

Among many friends, the names of two women in particular were prominent this year: Dulcie Hornby and Nora Farrell. The Hornby and Farrell homes were frequent venues for playing card games such as bridge or five hundred.

~

Went to Card Party at Hornby's. Played 5 hands of Five Hundred. Miss Gravely, Misses MacDonald, Suse, Dulcie, Fred Townley, Mr. Goodall, Teddy McLorg, Harold Marshall. Had a jolly time. Left about 12 o'clock. Feb. 23/09

Dulcie, Fred Townley & Goodall came in to tea. Dulcie stayed for dinner. Sun. Feb. 28/09

Went to Rowing Club Ball, got home 4:00 A.M. Took Dulcie H. Had supper with Dulcie & Miss Farrell. Apr. 16/09

Dulcie, Thompson, & Fred Townley came in, played bridge. Apr. 23/09

Bridge at Hornby's. Met Chrissie Smith who has just returned from Germany. Also met Babs MacPherson. The following were there: Blackwell, Teddy McLorg, Barwick, Harry Clyne, Faulding, Gordon Runkle, Thompson, Bull, Dulcie, May Leighton, Lilo Cuthbertson, Ruth Mills, Ruth P., Margot Gravely, Dot. Sept. 14/09

Went over to Miss Gradwell's at North Vancouver — had a jolly time. Sue, Dulcie, Betty Cameron, Miss

Butler, Mr. Wickem, Matthews, Simpson, Noel Hunt, Peplar. Sat. Oct. 2/09

Played Bridge at Marshall-Smith's. Gordon Runkle, Dulcie, Violet Ladner, Chrissie. Chrissie has just returned from Germany. She plays [piano] awfully well. They live corner of Nelson & Bidwell. Oct. 15/09

Took Susie, Gertie, Dulcie, Nora Farrell to Roller Rink — Sharpe came with us. Cost me 2.50. Had tea at Dulcie's afterwards. Mon. Nov. 8/09

Sue & I went to a 500 Party at the Farrell's, had a perfectly delightful time. They have a lovely home. The following people were there: Alice & Vi Ladner, The Tregent girls, Margot Whitney, Ruth Mills, Dulcie Hornby, Maude Kemp, Chrissie Marshall-Smith, Ted McLorg, Van Roggen, Peppler, Douglas, Boak, Thompson, Runkle, Sharpe. Dec. 16/09

~

Following the card party at the Farrell home on December 16, Christmas Day found Wallace, his sisters Sue and Gertie, Dulcie and her brother Geoff, and others, at a rugby game at Brockton Oval. Wallace closed the social part of 1909 by having another "lovely time" at a dance given by Peggy Hunt.

Cultural Activities

Wallace's love for the stage found him attending some of the wide range of cultural activities available in Vancouver in 1909, including opera, the symphony, and the Royal Italian Band. Instead of just listing what he had seen, this year he also started noting in his diary what he thought of the performances.

~

Went to see "Dolly Varden" at Opera house.
Feb. 18/09

Arthur & I went to see "Burgomaster". Not very good.
Mar. 1/09

Went to see "The Right Way". A very good play.
Apr. 8/09

With Edith to hear the International Grand Opera
Co. put on Cavaleria Rusticana & L. Pagliacci —
enjoyed it immensely. Sept. 24/09

A.L.B. & I went to hear Ellery's Band — Horse Show
Bldg. Very fine. The introductory to "Lohengrin" &
Paderewski's minuet were played magnificently. Also
Hungarian Rhapsody by Liszt. Oct./09

~

Outdoors
Wallace continued to enjoy canoe trips, camping, walking, and skating.

~

This has been a very cool summer. Paddled up to
Coombe with Lamphard last Saturday, came back
Sunday. Had a good time. Aug. 10/09

Paddled up North Arm with Arthur. Camped at
Whiskey Cove. Sept. 6/09 (Labour Day)

Arthur & I paddled up to Woodlands — took us 3
hours to go up — against the tide. Camped at Gould-
Smyth's Cottage. It was delightful. Sat. Sept. 25/09

~

Church
Wallace attended church regularly, appreciating both
the music and the social opportunities. In addition to
commenting on the quality of the music, he also began
making notes about the sermon and particularly
inspirational passages.

~

Search Thyself
Correct Thyself
Subdue Thyself.
Lytton in "Godolphin". Feb. 1909

Went to "At Home" given by Girls Auxiliary of St. John's
Church. Had very good time. Miss Hazel McLugan
sang — she has a very good voice. I noticed Mrs. C.J.
Peter, Miss Dallas, Miss Fraser, Miss Vista Fisher, The
Gibsons, Andersons, Boaks, Leckies, etc. Feb. 22/09

Went to recital in St. John's Church with Maude.
Madame Rosina Burke, Mrs. Saunders, Mr. Dean
Wells, Mr. Milne, Soloists. The choir sang Gauls "Holy
City" fairly well. Apr. 1/09

*Went to St. John's Church in the evening. Dr. Welch
preached a very good sermon. Easter Sunday
Apr. 11/09*

*I went to a Cantata in Christ Church. Eileen McGuire
sang beautifully, also Mrs. Coulthard & Conrad White.
Dec. 9/09*

~

Real Estate Investments

Land was fairly cheap in Vancouver at this time. Like
many ordinary wage-earners, Wallace and Maude, his
sister, lived in a rented house, but invested in real estate.
Maude was a trained nurse, and presumably employed,
and Wallace was earning $80 per month. The household
that Wallace and his sisters shared was likely supported
not only by Maude and Wallace, but also by Susan's
income. She was listed as an accountant for the Electrical
Department of the City of Vancouver. There was no
mention in the diary of Mary's occupation, nor of Gertie's.
Although Wallace never mentioned it, it was possible that
he and his sisters took in boarders to supplement the
household income. There was also no evidence in
Wallace's meticulously kept financial records that he
contributed to food for the household. This was no doubt
what allowed him enough disposable income both to
invest in real estate and to indulge in the many cultural
and social activities he so enjoyed.

~

*Maude & I paid 200.00 to Ralph Rademacher, 1/6
interest in lot 7 Blk 343 Broadway West Mon. Tue.
Oct. 26/09*

Made last payment on lot in Hastings. Nov. 17/09

~

Cecie

As in 1907, Wallace tersely mentioned Cecie's birthday on February 22. He made no further comment or mention of her name until August, when he dispassionately noted that he had received a letter from her. Did he reply? Yes, six weeks later, but gave no hint of what was said in either letter. Cecie's reply arrived in early December, but again Wallace did not mention the contents.

~

This is Cecie F.'s birthday, 21 years old today. Feb. 22/09

Had a letter from Cecie today. Aug. 10/09

10:30 P.M. Just finished writing a letter to Cecie. Sept. 21/09 (Rec. answer Dec. 2/09).

~

Notes

1. Evans, Coleman & Evans was a company dealing in building supplies. See the advertisement, this chapter. The company was situated at the Columbia Avenue wharf, at the foot of Columbia Street. The branch office was at 407 Granville Street. In 1908, the principals and their home addresses were: Ernest Edward Evans, 1075 Harwood Street; George Coleman, 1221 Burnaby Street; Percy Evans, 1273 Nelson Street.

Chapter 4

~

1910

"The Most Enjoyable Outing I Ever Had"

This was an eventful year indeed for Wallace. Although the spring marked a sudden death in his family, and at the end of the year, he joined the Reserve Army, the highlight of his year seemed to be a boating vacation he took with friends. As in previous years, his diary was mostly occupied with a round of outdoor, church, cultural, and social activities, but for the first time, he recorded some details about his work, and about the books he was reading.

Family

Late in April, tragedy struck the Chambers household when Wallace's sister, Mary, died after a massive internal haemorrhage. Wallace had made scant note of Mary prior to her death. After chronicling the course of her illness,[1] his diary never mentioned her again.

~

Mary took very ill at 6:15 P.M. Haemorrhage of stomach. Dr. Munro attending. Friday Apr. 22nd/10

Mary very weak. Great loss of blood. Sat. Apr. 23rd/10

Mary very weak all day. Sleeping under influence of morphine. Miss Whitehead came on duty this P.M. Sun. Apr. 24th/10

Mary very weak, but doctor has hopes of recovery. Dr. Gillies, Dr. Munro consultation at 7 P.M. Mon. Apr. 25th/10

Dear Mary died at 3:30 this morning — very peacefully. Miss Whitehead attending. Rest dear Sister, thy work is o'er. Thy willing hands will toil no more. It is God's will it should be so; By His Command we all must go. from T.K. Tue. Apr. 26th/10

Funeral 2 P.M. Rev. Mr. MacGillivray officiating. Pall Bearers Brett Barwick, P.A. McLean, C.G. Thompson, Alfred Kay. Apr. 27th/10

~

MARY AMELIA CHAMBERS.

The death occurred in the city this morning of Mary Amelia Chambers, who entered into rest at the family residence, 1155 Georgia St. The deceased was the second daughter of the late S. W. Chambers and is survived by one brother and three sisters, with whom much sympathy will be felt in their bereavement. The funeral, which will be private, will take place on Wednesday at 2 p.m. from the above residence, Rev. A. J. MacGillivray officiating.

Mary's obituary notice,[2] *The Vancouver World*, April 26, 1910

Work

Wallace's few references to his daily work life were sometimes embellished by descriptions of the weather or social activities, such as meeting Leon Ladner[3] for breakfast.

~

Came down to office at 7 o'clock this A.M. It was beautifully clear and slightly frosty. The sunrise on the snow-capped mtns. across the Inlet was magnificent. Monday Jan. 31/10

Had Breakfast at the Europe with Leon Ladner. Wed. Feb. 2/10

~

In February, Wallace noted that he had been with Evans, Coleman & Evans for one year. A few months later, one of the principals of the firm left for England.

~

Have been in the employ of Evans Coleman & Evans 1 year today. Tue. Feb. 15/10

Mr. Farrell gave farewell dinner to the Evans at Vanc. Club. Sat. Oct. 15th/10

P.W. Evans left today on the 4 o'clock train for England. via San Francisco & New York. Tue. Oct. 18th/10

H.J. Evans left today for England where he is going to live. Sat. Nov. 5th/10

~

Real Estate Investments

Wallace was rather casual about his real estate transactions. Having made the final payment on a Hastings lot in November 1909, he sold it in March 1910 for $300. How much he paid for it was not clear. Then, in April, he purchased a double lot at 10th Avenue and Garden in the Grandview area of Vancouver for $1,750. He did not mention whether his sister, Maude, was investing this year, although shortly after Mary's death, Maude took a secure and well-paid position with the law firm of Ridley & McRae.

~

Went out to look at Real Estate with Arthur. Bo't a double corner from Chas. E. Smith, 10th & Garden. $1,750.00. Sat. Apr. 2nd/10

Paid for my share of re surveying Grandview lot — $3.75. Total cost $15.00. Sat. July 30th/10

~

Outdoors

By 1910, Wallace had many friends with whom to share his love of the outdoors, and these activities became very much part of his social life.

~

*Went to Roller Skating Club. Skated with Sue, Nora &
Dulcie. Kathleen Judge was there. The girls served tea
at the rink. Jan. 20/10*

Walked to Second Beach. Sun. Feb. 6/10

*Arthur & I walked up the Capilano — lovely day.
Sat. Mar. 5th/10*

*Paddled up the Inlet — took Peggy Lucas-Hunt. Noel
& Sue, Brett & Gertie, Davies, Gordon Wickham,
Gwen, L. Jenkinson, Emily Irwin. Had a picnic.
Started to rain at noon. We got soaked. Had a rather
good time though. Tue. May 24th/10*

*Paddled up North Arm with Percy MacLean. Went to
Barwick's House. Sue & Gertie, Lucas-Hunt were
there — also Noel and Brett. Had a fine time.
Sat. June 18/10*

*Stayed all night. Rained heavily in morning. Started
home at 6 P.M., arrived 9 P.M. Lovely clear evening.
Sun. June 19/10*

～

Wallace had a twenty-five dollar canoe, and knew
some pretty girls who enjoyed the water on a summer's
evening. From one of them — someone he unfortunately
found "boring" — he even received a personalized canoe
cushion. He also took his sisters, Gertie and Sue, on some
of his "paddles." Wallace's friends, the Townleys, had a
launch, and that, too, provided many hours of outdoor
socializing.

～

*Got off at 10 A.M., went to Indian River with the
Townleys on their Launch "Edith", to see the Regatta.
Had a jolly time. Besides the Townley's there were:
Eileen Green, Janet Tupper, Miss Tupper, Violet
Walker, Miss Ruddick, Heb Green, Garland, Storey,
Higgins. Got home midnight. Fri. July 8th/10*

*Walked down with Clare Battle this morning. Asked
her to go canoeing. 8:00 P.M. Took Clare Battle
canoeing. Enjoyed it immensely. She is awfully nice.
Wed. July 13th/10*

*8:30 P.M. Took Peggy canoeing. Lovely night — full
moon but she bores me awfully. Wed. July 20th/10*

*Took Peggy Lucas-Hunt paddling Seymour Creek.
Noel took Agnes Squires. Billy & Mac took Kitty Allen.
Enjoyed it — the day was perfect. Got home 11:15 P.M.
Sun. July 24th/10*

Took Gertie & Sue canoeing. Wed. July 27th/10

*Gertie & I walked down to Park. Took some snap
shots. Sat. August 6th/10*

*Peggy gave me a canoe cushion with my initial on —
which she made. Wed. Sept. 21st/10*

～

In mid-August, with Fred Townley and others, Wallace
left for a ten-day vacation on the Townley family yacht,
"Edith." Starting at Vancouver's Coal Harbour, they
stopped at Bowen Island, Sechelt, Buccaneer Bay, and
Secret Cove, then back to Gibson's Landing, Bowen

Island, and into Indian Arm, to the Wigwam Inn. There Wallace caught the commercial ship, *Beaver,* returning him to Vancouver. Among the many highlights of the trip, Wallace appreciated the "big feeds," which in one instance consisted of pork and beans, peas and rice.

～

Wallace Chambers (standing) and Fred Townley, 1910

Started on cruise on the Townley's boat "Edith", left Coal Harbour 3 P.M. Bowen Island 5:30 P.M. Dance in evening. Met Nancy Vandin. Tue. Aug. 16th/10

Left 9:30 A.M. Lovely day. Arrived Sechelt. Left for Buccaneer Bay. Kathleen Smith & Plommer coming aboard. Aug. 17th/10

Spent day in Cove Edith. Left 6:00 P.M. for Secret Cove. Castor Oil for the Crew after a big feed. Fri. Aug. 19th/10

Secret Cove. Strong South Easterly blowing. Watched logging — Green & Clark's Camp. Sat. Aug. 20th/10

Strong South Easterly. Couldn't get out till evening — left 5 P.M. Very rough. Arrived Shelter Islands 9:30 P.M. Big feed. Sun. Aug. 21/10

Left 11 A.M., ran over to Gibson's Landing & then to Bowen Island. Dance in the evening. Took Nancy

canoeing. Supper afterwards at Mrs. Kirby's. Mon.
Aug. 22nd/10

Left for Indian River 5 P.M. Called at Camp Linger-
longer (the Campbells) had supper. Dance & played
Bridge. Gladys Campbell & Miss Nellis.
Wed. Aug. 24th/10

Arrived Indian River 9:30 A.M. Beached the H.M.S.
"Edith". All hands painting ship. Had a peach of a
time. All kinds of swearing and paint in evidence.
Floated at 7 P.M., ate a tremendous supper of Pork &
Beans, peas & rice. Thurs. Aug. 25th/10

12 noon — cloudy. Ran up to Wigwam Inn where I
left the "Edith", came down to town on the "Beaver"
after the most enjoyable outing I ever had.
Fri. Aug. 26th/10

~

Books

Wallace began to record the books he read, and
sometimes what he thought of them. He found Robert
Chambers' *The Danger Mark* "rather interesting," Charles
Read's *The Cloister and the Hearth* "awfully good," and
Florence Barclay's *The Rosary* "a very good story." Also in
this year, since reading was an interest they shared, he
and Cecie began exchanging books.

Cultural Activities

Wallace loved plays and music, and had no shortage of
companions. His diary was a compendium of the many
cultural activities happening in Vancouver at the time. This
year he recorded attending twenty-nine such functions at

venues including the Orpheum, the Empress Theatre, and
the Opera House.[4] He heard Harry Lauder sing and saw
Louis James play in *Henry VIII*. He enjoyed "Madame
Pavlova & Mordkin the Russian Dancers" at the Opera
House, mentioning the "fine orchestra" and the "magnificent
performance," and pronounced "The Witching Hour"
starring John Mason "awfully good."

~

*A Party of us went to the Empress Theatre to see
"Sweet Nell of Old Drury". Enjoyed it immensely.
Went to the Lucas-Hunt's for supper afterwards. Noel
Hunt, Peggy Hunt & myself, Mr. Waldo, Mr. Biggs,
Rita Biggs, Winnie Ridley who is a jolly nice girl
visiting here from England, Essex Co. Thur. Jan 13/10*

*Maude, Mary & I went to hear Madam Shuman
Heinck. She has a magnificent voice and lovely
personality. Fri. Mar. 4th/10*

*Geoffrey Sharpe & I went to see the "Stubborn
Cinderella". Homer Mason leading man. He was
good. Wed. Mar. 16/10*

*At Edith's for Dinner. Arthur & I went to hear Mark
Hambourg, Pianist. He played Mendelsohn's
Wedding March magnificently. Jampolski (Baritone)
sang awfully well. Tue. Mar. 22/10*

*Geoff & I went to see the "Red Mill". Rotten show. Had
supper afterward at Dutch Grill. Wed. Apr. 13/10*

Saturday evening Arthur & I went to see Mantell play in "King Lear". He is a very clever actor. Miss Booth Russell was splendid. Sat. Apr. 16/10

Mr. & Mrs. Montagu Burge, Middleton & Ker, Sue, Gertie, Maude & myself went to the Theatre Party at the Empress to see the "Mysterious Burglar". Rather good. Very funny at times. Tues. Sept. 13th/10

Wilkie & I went to see Hackett in "Monsieur Beaucaire" at the Opera House. He is a good actor. I enjoyed it but Wilkie didn't like it. Tues. Oct. 25th/10

Mac & I went to see DeWolf Hopper in "The Matinee Idol". Rather good. Sat. Nov. 12th/10

~

Church

Wallace continued to record the highlights — and low points in the case of one singer — of church concerts and sermons. Clare Battle, a journalist, accompanied him to hear the *Messiah* at the end of the year. Her newspaper account (which Wallace saved in his diary) echoed Wallace's enthusiasm for the evening, except for one jarring note. She wrote: "If there was a marring feature, it was the fact that applause was allowed, or if not allowed, at least countenanced."

~

Took Edith to Sacred Concert in Christ's Church. Miss Coulthard sang beautifully. H.J. Cave's voice hasn't improved. Thurs. Jan. 27/10

Went to Church. Mrs. Coultard sang "Angels Ever Bright." Fair. Sun. Mar. 6th/10

7 P.M. and went to church in the evening. Dr. McKay preached a very good sermon. Sunday Mar. 27/10

Mr. White preached a very good sermon in St. John's. Mrs. Coulthard, Mr. Milne sang a duet "Oh Love Divine". Sun. Apr. 10/10

Choir sang "Hear My Prayer" very well. Mrs. Coulthard sang the solo part divinely. Sun. May 8th/10

Professor Pidgeon preached an excellent sermon in St. John's. Sun. July 10th/10

Clare & I went to hear the "Messiah" in St. John's Church. H.J. Cave tenor, Mrs. Coulthard soprano, Ellen Maguire contralto, G. Hicks Bass, and chorus of 90. They sang it very well. Thurs. Dec. 29th/10

~

Social Activities

Wallace's social calendar remained full with dances, at-homes, card-playing, teas, and meals in restaurants. His diary entries for January, February, and March were typical of the number of social activities in which he was an enthusiastic participant.

~

Mrs. Farrell gave a Children's Party in the Granville Mansion — I went and had a glorious time, had afternoon tea in Dutch Grill. The other grown-ups were: Dulcie Hornby, Nora Farrell, Kathleen Wilson, Margot Whitney, Maude Tregent, Chrissie Smith, Runkle, Thompson, Ladner, Dr. Wilson, Smythe, Horace Smith. Sat. Jan. 8/10

Went to Arcadia Club Dance in Lester Hall. Had a jolly time. Peggy Hunt asked me up to their place for Bridge but I had an engagement and couldn't accept. Met K. Smith. Jan. 11/10

Went to the Orpheum with Sue, Gertie, & Dulcie. Dulcie was at our place for dinner. Wed. Jan. 12/10

Went to Ball given by Daughters of the Empire — got home at 3:30 A.M. Fri. Jan. 14/10

Sue & I went to dance at "Craiglockhart" Georgia St., had a perfectly delightful time — met Kathleen Judge who is awfully sweet. Got home 2 A.M. Tue. Jan. 18th/10

Went to Roller Skating Club. Skated with Sue, Nora & Dulcie. Kathleen Judge was there. The girls served tea at the rink. Thurs. Jan. 20/10

Farrell's Dance in the Granville Mansions — had a peach of a time. Met Kathleen Wilson, Miss Nora Thompson, Miss Muriel Colls, Gertrude Nichol (for the first time). Got home 3:00 A.M., in a taxi. We had supper in the Dutch Grill — Faulding, Margot Whitney, Dulcie & I supped together. Fri. Jan. 21/10

Club Dance. Jolly time. Met Clare Battle & Miss Nichol. Went home with Muriel Colls in a taxi. Nora

Farrell is awfully nice. Gordon Runkle took Sue &
Gertie in a taxicab. Tue. Jan. 25/10

~

Typical of the day, the following *Vancouver World*[5]
newspaper clipping which Wallace saved in his diary
listed everyone who was at an Arcadia Club dance he
attended on February 8, 1910. Wallace described the
dance this way: *"Took Dulcie to Club Dance, the last*
before Lent. Met Mrs. Godson, wife of Captain Godson —
charming. Got home 1:30."

ARCADIA CLUB DANCE

The Arcadia Club met last evening in the Lester Hall for
the last time before Easter. In honour of the occasion,
dancing was kept up till one o'clock, the guests having the
use of the large hall for the hour after midnight. Among
those present were Mr. and Mrs. Makovski, Mr. and Mrs.
Edgerton, Mr. and Mrs. Nichol, Captain and Mrs. Godson,
Miss Mellish, Miss Kemp, Miss Kathleen Smith, Miss Emily
Irwin, Miss Lucas Hunt, Miss Alexander, Miss Dulcie Hornby,
Miss Battle, Miss Chambers, Miss Binnington, the Misses
Burpee, Miss Butler (North Vancouver), Miss Fraser, Miss
Fitzpatrick Smith, Messrs. Curtis, Benham, Smyth, Rigg,
Fraser, Chambers, Maitland, Crosier, Wickham, Popham,
Thornton, Runkle, Jardine.

~

Bridge at Violet Gradwell's. Nora Farrell, Dulcie
Hornby, Chrissie Smith, Lilo Cuthbertson, Thompson,
Runkle, Pepler, Butler. Chrissie & I beat Thompson &
Lilo 624-146. We made 2 grand slams. Fri. Feb. 25/10

Bridge at Mrs. Walkem's. Lilo Cuthbertson, Sally
Danis, Dulcie Hornby, Chrissie Marshall-Smith,

Maisie Campbell-Johnson, Margot Whitney, Nora
Farrell, Mr. Jarvis, Mr. Gorst, Gavin Davis, Runkle,
W. Marshall. Fine time. I won the booby prize.
Thurs. Mar. 3rd/10

This is Dulcie's birthday (23). We gave her a surprise
party. Played progressing 500. Chrissie Smith, Lilo
Cuthbertson, Sally Davis, Sue, Gertie, Margot Whitney,
Nora Farrell, Ch. Thompson, Gordon Runkle,
W. Marshall, Naylor, W. James. Sat. Mar. 5th/10

~

On April 7, Wallace recorded that his friend, Burge,
took "A.M.C." to an event at the Orpheum. "A.M.C." could
have referred either to Wallace's sister, Maude, or to his
sister, Mary, who would die just nineteen days later.

~

Took Sue & Gertrude to a Dance No. Vanc. Burge
took A.M.C. to Orpheum. Thurs. Apr. 7th/10

Arcadian Club Dance, Lester Hall. Awfully good
time. Clare Battle is very nice. Very fine looking.
Went home with Dulcie. Fri. Apr. 8th/10

Box Party at Pantages. Arthur, Burge & I; Sue, Edith,
Maude, Gertie. Enjoyed it immensely. Sat. Apr. 9th/10

Chrissie Marshall-Smith invited me to a Bridge &
Dance at her place for Friday evening. Accepted.
Tue. Apr. 12/10

Went to a dance at the Marshall-Smiths. Played "500" first. Had a very good time. Van Roggen, Douglas, Ted McLorg, Leon Ladner, Casement, G. William, Dr. Wilson, Pepler, Thompson, Runkle, Sharpe. Nora Farrell, Lilo Cuthbertson, Margot Gravely, Margot Whitney, Maude Tregent, Rhona Bain, Sue, Gertie, Dulcie, Gladys Lord, Gwen. Got home 3 A.M. Fri. Apr. 15/10

~

With a brief period of mourning after Mary died on April 26, Wallace's social activities continued unabated.

~

Went in the Farrell's Launch "Noriensha" to Bedwell Bay. Nora Farrell, Chrissie Smith, Margot Whitney, Dulcie Hornby, Van Roggen, Gordon, Mr. & Mrs. F. Gramophone aboard — had a delightful walk through the wood to Belcarra. When we got in we went to the Farrell's for 9 o'clock supper.
Sun. May 22nd/10

Gordon Runkle came in last night. We played Baccarat. We stuck him for chocolates.
Thur. May 26th/10

Played Bridge at the Marshall-Smith's. Walked home with Dulcie. Tupper's Dance. Fri. May 27/10

On Sunday we were going out with Lucas-Hunts, but it rained — so went up to their place for lunch. Mrs. & Miss Vivi Mudge from Montreal were there, also Kitty Allen, Gladys Turner, Brett Barwick, Archie

Field, Lee Waldo. We stayed all afternoon, had tea at 4:30. Sun. June 5th/10

Went to Garden Party at the Lucas-Hunt's. Mrs. Arthur Ray, Miss V. Mudge, Miss Kemp, Miss Squires, Miss Barwick, Drayton, Waldo, Field, Lee, Brett Barwick. Wed. June 29/10

Evening at Hornby's. Mr. Davies, Ruth, Chrissie, Mr. Douglas. Played Bridge. Sue & Gertie went to Theatre with Mr. Ker & Middleton. Mr. Tytler asked to a Bridge at their place tomorrow evening. Tytler is awfully clever with the brush. He has done some lovely water colours and oils. Wed. Sept. 28th/10

Raining. 4 P.M. went to Tea at the Hunt's. Rita & Hattie Biggs were there, also Mr. Goodall & Jimmy Underhill. Yesterday was Peggy's birthday. Sun. Oct. 16th/10

~

This year, Wallace's diary was filled with notations like: *"Kathleen Judge is awfully sweet,"* and *"Nora Farrell is awfully nice."* In addition to his sisters and Dulcie Hornby, the names of several other women appeared often in Wallace's diary. These included Clare Battle, Eugenie Brünn, and Mrs. Schwengers from Victoria.

Wallace first noted Clare Battle at a dance in December 1909, but did not actually meet her until January 1910. More than two months later, he recorded, *"Clare Battle is very nice, very fine looking,"* and by December 31, wrote: *"I'm growing more fond of her every day."* At the first of the Rowing Club dances for the season, Wallace escorted Clare home. This may have meant her acceptance to dance with him the romantic last dance in a darkened hall, and perhaps to hold hands on the way home, with a good-night kiss. In 1910, did romance proceed that swiftly?

In any event, Clare consented to be escorted home again after another dance, and gave Wallace her photo. Clare and Wallace saw each other frequently in 1910, often accompanied by Clare's brother, Arthur. That Wallace showed no resentment about the younger brother's presence suggested either a magnanimous temperament, or the absence of a strong romantic attachment.

Perhaps Wallace's relationship with Clare was platonic, but this description appeared even more applicable to his relationship with Dulcie Hornby, who was close to his sister, Sue, and part of a wide circle of friends that included Nora Farrell, Chrissie Marshall-Smith, and Peggy Lucas-Hunt. But at Chrissie Marshall-Smith's "At Home" dance in November, he met Eugenie Brünn, a young Norwegian woman with "a very pretty accent." Her name began to appear frequently in his diary, and would continue to do so for the next few years.

Wallace's 1910 Vancouver Rowing Club
membership card

Smith's Dance was very jolly. Met Miss Brünn first time. She is Norwegian with a very pretty accent. Clara Lord is charming. Tomorrow is Chrissie's birthday. Left at 2:15 A.M. Wed. Nov. 16th/10

3 P.M. took Eugenie Brünn for a walk to the Country Club — afterwards had tea at the Ritz. Sun. Dec. 11th/10

Took Eugenie to the Orpheum. Sat in a box. She is going to write me a note in Norwegian. Lovely clear night. Stars shining. Got home 1 A.M. Fri. December 23rd 1910

2:30 went to see Rugby. Vanc. beat Stanford 13-6. Took Dulcie, Eugenie, Sue, Guy, Arthur, & Gavin — dinner at Edith's at 7:30. Mon. Dec. 26th/10

~

In February, first at the Girls Auxiliary Ball, and the next night at the Ladies Hockey Club Ball, Wallace met the "lovely" and "charming" Mrs. Schwengers from Victoria. A newspaper clipping (which Wallace saved) noted that the dance by the Vancouver Ladies Hockey Club was held in honour of the visiting Victoria club and that "Among the Victoria guests noticed was Mrs. Schwengers." After that night, no matter who accompanied Wallace to an event, he often noted whether Mrs. Schwengers was present.

~

Took Violet Gradwell to the Girls Auxiliary Ball in Lester Hall. Met Mrs. Schwengers from Victoria (lovely). Friday Feb. 4, 1910

*Went to Ladies Hockey Club dance in Granville
Mansions. Mrs. Schwengers was much admired.
Walked home with Dulcie 1 A.M.
Saturday Feb. 5, 1910*

*Geoff Sharp & I met "City of Puebla". Mrs. Schwengers
and the Misses Smith were aboard. Mrs. Schwengers
invited me to a picnic in Victoria next week-end, but
I couldn't accept. Sat. July 25/10*

*Asked Dulcie to go to the Daughters of the Empire
Ball. Chrissie is coming with us. Met Mrs. Schwengers
on train. Wed. Nov. 2/10*

*Daughters of the Empire Ball, Lester Hall. Took
Dulcie & Chrissie. Had a ripping time. Got home 3
A.M. Mrs. S. was charming — . Thurs. Nov. 3/10*

*Dance in honour of Stanford Football Team. Took
Clare. Mrs. S. was there. Saturday Dec. 31/10*

Christmas card, one side signed by Wallace and the other signed by family
members and friends sharing Christmas dinner at his home that year.
Wallace's diary entry read: *"This has been a very happy Xmas. We had ten in
for supper— went to St. John's in the evening. Dec. 25/10"*

Wallace saved a clipping of Clare Battle's social column in the *Vancouver World,* in which she wrote an account of the New Year's Eve dance they attended together. After outlining the activities of the evening (as shown in the excerpt below), Clare listed everyone who attended and described briefly what the women were wearing. Pale pink silk seemed to be the most popular dress colour and fabric.

NEW YEAR'S EVE DANCE

One of the jolliest gatherings ever held in the Lester Hall took place on Saturday evening, New Year's Eve, when the Vancouver Rowing Club Football Team entertained in honour of the visiting Stanford team. Few pleasanter ways of memorializing the death of the Old Year and the birth of the New could have been imagined, and those who enjoyed the hospitality of the Rowing Club men will remember the evening for a long time to come. . . .

The floor was perfect as only the Lester Hall floor can be, and the music, as supplied by Mr. Harpur and his talented orchestra, was among the best that has ever been heard in the city, the programme appropriately containing some well known American national airs. The only thing to be regretted was the scarcity of ladies, which made dancing impossible for a large number of the men present.

The programme was kept up until five minutes before the hour of midnight. Then as the last strains of the Songe l'Automne and Home Sweet Home waltz died away, a fanfare beat out a requiem for the old year and a welcome for the infant 1911. Hands were joined and the dancers forming one huge circle moved slowly round the spacious ballroom which has been the scene of so many happy gatherings, singing Auld Lang Syne. Then followed the national anthem and after that, those present trooped down to supper, New Year greetings being heard on every side. . . .

Cecie

Wallace was surrounded by female pulchritude, and seemed to be in an enviable position with respect to his romantic life. Despite this, he found time to communicate with Cecie, a young woman he had met briefly five years previously. Though Wallace divulged little in his diary about his feelings, he and Cecie were having some significant communication by letter. As usual, he noted her February birthday, but in addition, throughout this year he recorded writing and receiving a number of letters. In July, he noted that he had not heard from Cecie lately, and acknowledged: *"I guess because I have not written."* In October, after receiving from Cecie a set of books, *Lovely Woman*, he replied the next day, and enclosed a few photographs. This year, he sent Cecie a Christmas letter, and an Armenian lace handkerchief.[6]

Military Activities

On December 16, Wallace was sworn into the Reserve Army, the 72nd Highlanders.[7] He may or may not have been motivated by a bit of tradition. At the age of twenty-five, Wallace's father had been commissioned as an ensign in the Number Two Company of the 19th "Lincoln" Battalion. Wallace's grand-father, William Chambers, who was a farmer at Woodstock, Upper Canada, had been a captain in the Number Seven Company of the 22nd "The Oxford Rifles" Volunteer Battalion.

∼

Wrote to Capt. Godson re 72rd Canadian Highlanders. Fri. Dec. 9th/10

Cap't Godson asked me to take a commission in the 72nd Canadian Highlanders. I would like to very

much, but can't afford it — would cost about
$300.00 Mon. Dec. 12th/10

6:15 Met Gavin — had dinner with him at MacIntyre's.
7:00 P.M. Went up to Western Club. Met Kay. We
went to the Armouries & joined the 72nd Highlanders.
Fri. Dec. 16th/10

8:00 P.M. Sworn into the 72nd Highlanders —
passed doctor's examination. My height is 6 ft. 2 3/4"
in boots, chest 38 1/2". Sat. Dec. 17/10

~

Notes

1. The doctors who treated Mary were Dr. Alexander Stewart Munro and
    Dr. Digby Gillies. Dr. Munro, a surgeon, was born in Scotland on May 1,
    1872. He was educated at Toronto and Winnipeg public schools, and
    attended university in Manitoba, Chicago, and Vienna. Dr. Munro moved
    to British Columbia in 1896, and established a medical practice with
    Drs. Bryden-Jack and Cumming. Dr. Digby Gillies was born in Ontario on
    June 11, 1875, and moved to British Columbia in 1900, having graduated
    from Montreal's McGill Medical College. His brother, Ernest, was also a
    physician. Their office in 1910 was at 510 Granville Street in Vancouver.

    Mary appears to have died from a bleeding peptic ulcer. You may
    wonder why she was not put into hospital, given blood transfusions, and
    so on. In 1910, this was still highly experimental, and not a consideration.
    Her treatment reflects the information found in Sir William Osler's *The
    Principles and Practice of Medicine* (8th edition, New York and London,
    D. Appleton and Company, 1912), the pre-eminent medical textbook of
    that era, which outlined the treatment to be absolute bed rest, diet, and
    "morphia for pain." Only a passing nod was offered to blood transfusions:
    "transfusion may be necessary, or still better, the subcutaneous infusion
    of saline."

    The problems of incompatibility had been recognized, but only
    recently, and doctors had not learned how to prevent the blood from
    clotting after it was taken from the donor. In 1914, it was discovered that
    sodium citrate (still used today in 1998) was effective as an anticoagulant.
    In 1917 and 1918 came the first descriptions of transfusing stored blood,
    with success on the battlefield. This was too late to save Wallace from the
    fatal haemorrhage he suffered after being struck in the thigh by a sniper's
    bullet in 1915.

2. Mary was survived by four sisters, not by three as the obituary stated.

3. According to the Vancouver Registry, Leon Ladner was a law student
    living at 1018 Bidwell Street.

4. The Orpheum Theatre of pre-World War I was distinct from the present-
    day structure, which was built in 1927 on Smithe at Seymour in Vancouver.
    In 1908, the Orpheum Theatre's address was listed as 805 Pender Street.
    In 1910, the Empress Theatre was located at 276 Hastings Street. The
    Vancouver Opera House was built in 1891 at 759 Granville Street. After
    1912, it became successively the Orpheum, the Vancouver Theatre, the
    Lyric Theatre, and the International Cinema.

5. *The Vancouver World* was a precursor to today's *The Vancouver Sun*. (For
    more information, see p. 420, *The Greater Vancouver Book* by Chuck
    Davis, editor-in-chief, Linkman Press, 15032 - 97th Avenue, Surrey, B.C.,
    1997.) Unfortunately, the originals of this and the other newspaper
    clippings used in this book are too fragile, too long, or too discoloured to
    be reproduced here exactly.

6. Cecie's Armenian lace handkerchief was itemized in Wallace's December cash account.

7. In the meantime, thousands of miles away in the Balkans, there was ongoing political and social ferment which would soon have grave consequences for Wallace and his generation. For the interested reader, I recommend the *Chronicle of the World* (Chronicle Communications Ltd., London, published in 1989 in Australia, Canada and New Zealand by JL International Publishing Inc., 244 Mill Street, Liberty, Maryland 64068).

Chapter 5

~

1911

"Appointed Sergeant 72nd Highlanders"

This year Wallace was promoted to sergeant and military activities began to take up more of his time. He also received a promotion at work, and continued his real estate transactions. In Wallace's household, one sister became engaged, and another turned twenty-one, and therefore could be included in more of Wallace's social activities. He continued to attend many cultural functions, and for the first time mentioned "moving pictures," a new theatre, Vancouver's first artificial ice rink, and "motoring." He enjoyed a summer vacation crewing on a friend's yacht, but had fewer marathon canoeing adventures, choosing brief and perhaps romantic canoe trips. And, although the names of several women friends still figured prominently in Wallace's diary, his correspondence with faraway Cecie continued to flourish.

Work
As always, Wallace's references to his work were scarce, but he did note that he had received a promotion to Assistant Sales Manager with Evans, Coleman & Evans.

Although he did not mention whether an immediate boost in salary accompanied this honour, at Christmas he received some extra funds.

~

Promoted Ass't Sales Manager, Evans, Coleman & Evans Ltd. Friday Sept. 1st/11

Got $50.00 Xmas bonus from the firm, also a raise of 15.00 per month. Fri. Dec. 2nd/11

~

Real Estate Investments
Wallace was still buying and selling real estate in Vancouver's "hot" market. By October, with Arthur as co-owner, Wallace had made the final payment on the lot at 10th Avenue and Garden, which he had bought in 1910.

~

Walked out with Arthur to see our lot on 10th & Garden. Thurs. July 6th/11

~

Wallace wrote about another property, at 1423 Cotton Drive, which he sold to H. H. Blanchet, presumably Arthur's brother. In the meantime, he and Maude had one-sixth of a share in a lot on Broadway, between Vine and Balsam, but owed another $200 due September 1912.

Church

Throughout this year, Wallace continued to be a faithful church-goer, most often to St. John's Church, but occasionally to St. James Church. Sometimes he was accompanied by one of his sisters — Edith or Maude — and sometimes by Clare Battle or Eugenie Brünn. Most of his church entries this year simply name the speaker; more rarely, as in the entry below, he commented favourably on what he considered to be good preaching.

~

Went to hear Herbert Booth in Wesley Church. He preaches awfully well. Very dramatic.
Mon. Jan. 23rd/11

~

Outdoors

Alone or with others, walking and canoeing remained among Wallace's most frequently mentioned outdoor activities.

~

Gavin & I went for a walk to Shaughnessy Heights — a lot of building is going on there. Had tea at the Tea Kettle. Fun. Sat. Feb. 25th/11

Had lunch at Edith's & Arthur's — & walked to Point Grey. Sun. Feb. 26th/11

3:30 Cut the lawn. 4 P.M. Walked in Stanley Park. Sat. May 6th/11

2:30 Walked out to the Wireless Station, Point Grey.
Sat. May 13th/11

Walked to Lynn Valley with Geo Kay, Egerton, Sue,
Dulcie, & Hattie Biggs. Sun. May 21st/11

Middleton & I went boating in the afternoon. He and
Robertson stayed at our place for supper.
Sunday June 4th/11

3 P.M. Mowed the Lawn, trimmed the hedge.
9:30 Walked to English Bay with Arthur. Lovely night.
Sat. June 10th/11

Raining. Canoeing with Arthur & Mac.
Sat. July 1st/11

~

In July, Wallace's friend, Gordon Runkle, asked him to
go on a seven-day yachting vacation with a group of
other friends. They sailed from Bowen Island north to
Powell River, west across the Strait of Georgia to Comox,
south to Nanaimo, than east back to Vancouver. Wallace
pronounced it "a most enjoyable week."

~

Quite hot. 8 P.M. Started on a week's holiday on
Gordon Runkle's yacht the "Canuck". Got to Bowen
Island first night. Sat. July 15th/11

Strong wind broke back-stay — repaired at Gibson's
Landing. Stayed there all night. Sun. July 16th/11

Lovely weather. Sailed for Pender Harbour. Arrived 8 P.M. Mon. July 17th/11

Weather fine & hot. Left Pender Harbour 7:15 A.M. Powell River 2 P.M. Savory Island 6 P.M. Lundy 8:30 P.M. Tue. July 18th/11

Left Lundy 7:30 A.M. Crossed the gulf to Comox, had a fine wind and sailed 7 mi. per hour. Comox is very pretty. Wed. July 19th/11

Strong head wind (Easterly). Started at noon. Sailed to Fanny Bay, arrived 8 P.M. Thurs. July 20/11

7:30 Left Fanny Bay under power for Nanaimo. Put into Nanoose Harbour for the night. Got bread at Wallace's ranch. Fri. July 21/11

Very hot. Left 7:00 A.M. Reached Nanaimo 6:00 P.M. Caught 7 big salmon. Crew all very sun-burned. Sat. July 22nd/11

Left 7 A.M. Fair wind. Crossed gulf to Bowen Island in 5 hours. Went swimming. Arrived Vancouver 6:30 P.M. after a most enjoyable week. Sun. July 23rd/11

~

In December, Wallace tried the new artificial ice rink for the first time.

~

*9 P.M. R.C. Hockey Club meeting. 11 P.M. First
Hockey practice on the new artificial ice surface with
the Vancouver Rowing Club team. Tue. Dec. 26th/11*

~

Cultural Activities

Wallace's cultural activities were a reflection of the
wide variety of Vancouver's cultural events. Such venues
as the Pantages Theatre, the Orpheum, and the Opera
House were attracting world-class performers.

MME. TETRAZZINI AT OPERA HOUSE

If no floral tributes fell to the lot of
Mme. Tetrazzini last evening upon her
first appearance in Vancouver there at
least awaited her the full-hearted ho-
mage of a vast audience whose enthusiasm was expressed in a perfect furore
of applause that came with spontaneous
response at the close of each of her
marvellous flights of bravura singing.
It is a tour de force of art, indeed, to
touch the zenith of coloratura singing in
the elaborate broderies of each of her
well-known arias from Verdi, Donizetti,
Mozart and Rossini, and still greater
to add, as Mme. Tetrezzini invariably
did, to each group; yet another number as a gracious acknowledgment of
the insistent applause that greeted her.
Most notable, perhaps, was her singing
of the "mad scene" from Lucia di Lam-
meroor, where her dazzling staccato
notes, her brilliant high tones and the
facility with which runs and trills were
executed, showed the range and unique
qualities of both voice and art.

Excerpt of a *Vancouver World* clipping, Jan. 12, 1911

In 1911, Wallace enjoyed a particularly rich cultural life, and combined cultural, social, and possibly romantic activities. In January alone, he took Eugenie Brünn to the Orpheum, Dulcie Hornby to the Empress, and Clare Battle to the Opera House! But lady friends were not his only companions — names such as Charley Smith, Wilkie, Gavin Tait-Ker, Mac, and Gerald appeared often.

~

Asked Dulcie to go to the Empress Tuesday to see the "Blue Mouse". Mon. Jan. 9th/11

Took Clare to hear Mme. Tetrazzini at the Opera house. Simply magnificent. Fred R. Hastings, Baritone; Andre Benoist, Pianist; Oesterreicher, Flutist. Thurs. Jan. 12th/11

Eugenie & I went to the Orpheum. Awfully good. Fri. Jan. 13th/11

Went to Pantages Theatre with Charley Smith (Vernon, B.C.). Supper at Rainier afterwards. Thurs. Feb. 9th/11

Theatre party at "Empress" — "The Message from Mars". Awfully well played. Mr. & Mrs. Egerton, Dulcie, Rita, Miss Fraser, Bullock-Webster, Kay, Littledale. Fri. Feb. 17th/11

Took Eugenie to hear the Canadian violinist Kathleen Parlow. She plays divinely. Sat. Feb. 25th/11

Took Miss Agnes Martin to see "The Missing Girl". Very good. Sue & Gavin went also. Mon. Feb. 27th/11

Wilkie & I heard Josef Hofman the great Pianist. Supper at the Carlton afterward. Fri. Mar. 3rd/11

Gavin & I went to see Edward Terry, the great English actor, in "Sweet Lavender". Awfully good play & he was supported by a splendid company. Mon. March 6th/11

Gavin Tait-Ker & I took Susie & Gertie to see Terry in "The Magistrate". My word! It is a pleasure to see good acting. Tue. Mar. 7th/11

Went to see Il Trovatore with Eugenie at the Maple Leaf. Sat. Mar. 11th/11

Lunched with Gavin. Went to hear Jinizadasa (Theosophist) lecture on Wagner's Tannhauser. Sun. Mar. 12th/11

Heard Signor Bonci the great Tenor. He sings nearly as well as Caruso. Fri. Mar. 17th/11

"The Arcadians" at the Opera House. Fine show. One of the best Musical Comedies I ever saw. Went with Wilkie. By Jove it was good. Supper at the Carleton afterwards. Fri. Mar. 24th/11

~

In the midst of a large number of entries about cultural events, what appeared to be a glitch: Wallace called for Eugenie, but ended up taking Dulcie to the Orpheum. Was Eugenie unavailable, so he took Dulcie instead? Such glitches hinted at the presence of drama in Wallace's own life; at the same time, his diary did not provide details, lurid or otherwise.

~

8:30 called at Glencoe Lodge for Eugenie 9:00 P.M.
took Dulcie to the Orpheum. Fri. Apr. 7th/11

8:30 Dr. Roland Dwight Grant's lecture on
Michaelangelo at the Opera House. Awfully good.
Michaelangelo was a wonderful man.
Tue. Apr. 11th/11

T.M. Wilkie, Maude & I went to hear Mincha Elinan
the great violinist at the Opera House.
Wed. Apr. 19th/11

8:30 went to Opera House to see "Madam Sherry".
Thurs. Apr. 27th/11

8:30 Went to the "Jessie McLaughlin" Concert.
Enjoyed it. She sings Scottish songs superbly.
Monday May 1st/11

Took Dulcie Hornby to see Frederick Warde & Players
in Shakespeare's "Julius Caesar". Awfully good.
Fri. May 5th/11

Sheffield Choir Concert. Magnificent. Went with my
three sisters. Lady Norah Noel sang Toski's "Good
Bye". Rob't Chignell has a superb Baritone voice.
They sang the Hallelujah chorus divinely.
Tue. May 16th/11

7 P.M. dinner at Dutch Grill with Foster & Kerr
afterwards to Theatre to see "The Winning Miss".
Fri. June 2nd/11

~

In June, Wallace recorded seeing a "moving picture."
This was his first mention of movies. Previous visits to the
theatre appeared to have been for plays.

~

Went to moving picture theatre with E.B. Saw Agnes
Martin there. Tue. June 27th/11

~

Wallace's friend, Gerald Heath,[1] was a music enthusiast
who had his own gramophone. Wallace added listening to
records to his cultural pleasures of the fall.

~

Heath brought his gramophone to our house. He has
some awfully good records — Caruso, Tetrazzini,
Melba, etc. Monday Oct. 9th/11

Went to Recital Christ Church. Mrs. Francis T.
Chambers contralto. Ferdinand Dunkley at the
organ. Sat. Oct. 14th/11

Saw Lawrence D'Orsay in "The Earl of Pawtuckett"
— "Awfully good donchaknow". Sat. Nov. 11th/11

8:30 Mac, Gerald Heath & I went to see "Old Town"
at the Opera House (Montgomery Stone). Very good.
Sat. Dec. 30th/11

~

Family

Wallace mentioned Gertie more frequently now that
she was twenty-one. He took her and sister Sue to several
events, including "Ye Dance Clubbe" on January 5
(*"Awfully jolly"*), to friends for tea, and to the theatre, and
often recorded the names of those who accompanied
Gertie and Sue to other events. For example, he recorded
that in May, Gertie and Mac went canoeing; in November,
Sue and Gertie went to a North Vancouver dance with
Gerald Heath and Mac; and in December, Middy (Wilfred
Middleton), an accountant at the Royal Bank of Canada
(*"who plays the piano very well"*), took Gertie to the Opera
House. Also in December, Wallace chaperoned Gertie to
the Lonsdale Hockey Club dance, where he found himself
enchanted by both pulchritude and charm.

~

Lonsdale Hockey Club dance. Very jolly. Miss Krupa
was there — she is exceedingly beautiful — met Miss
Roughton, a charming girl just out from London. I
took Gertie & Gwen. Home 2 A.M. Tue. Dec.19th/11

~

Like Wallace, sister Sue enjoyed quite an active social
life. Wallace's diary also noted some of her activities, and
the names of a number of young men, including Gavin
Tait-Ker, Brett Barwick, and Gerald Heath. After Sue's

twenty-third birthday, she became informally engaged to Fred Townley, son of a former mayor of Vancouver. [2] Wallace's diary entry was laconic about this news, although he seemed pleased to be invited to the Townley family's "At Home" dance in October. At that time, Wallace recorded that Fred had acquired a new "motor" in which he took Sue and Gertie for rides. In November, when Fred and Sue became formally engaged, Wallace's entry was again terse.

~

Susie's birthday. Gave her a hand made Irish Lace Collar. Wed June 26th/11

Fred Townley came up to our house. S.R.C. engaged F.L.T. Tue. June 27th/11

Got Mrs. T.O. Townley's invitation for "At Home" at Glencoe Lodge on 17th. It will be very swagger. Monday Oct. 2nd/11

Fred came in. Sue engaged to Fred Townley. Nov. 7/11

~

Social Activities

This year Wallace again saw a lot of Dulcie Hornby, often with other friends. Her home was a frequent venue for gatherings for bridge or tea, and she continued to be Wallace's frequent companion for outings. Dulcie was a close friend of Sue, and went to the Chambers home for dinner many times. One night while she dined with the Chambers family, Wallace's sister, Edith, and her daughter,

Phyllis, also paid a visit, yet Wallace took time to meet Clare Battle, and to phone Eugenie Brünn. In his diary, Wallace was not forthcoming about whether his relationship with Dulcie was romantic, but it was clear that just as he went to events with other women friends, Dulcie went to events with other men friends. Whatever Wallace's feelings, Dulcie's name appeared many times throughout 1911.

~

4:30 P.M. Tea at Dulcie's. Nora Farrell, Lilo Cuthbertson, Rita Biggs, Sue, Gertie, Margot Whitney, T. Kay, Ted Matthews, Gordon Wickham. Jan. 8/11

Went with Dulcie to a Bridge at the McFeely's, Burnaby St. Met Jean McGillivray, Nina Francis, Mrs. Dewar. Wed. Jan. 18th/11

Spent the evening at the Hornby's. Lilo, Rita, Sue, Gertie, Kay, Harold, O'Keefe, Kerr. Played Bridge. Mon. Jan. 30th/11

Surprise party for Dulcie. 5 tables of Bridge. Sat. Mar. 4th/11

Dulcie's birthday (24). Sun. Mar. 5th/11

Lovely day. Tea at Mrs. Burton-Brooke's with Dulcie. Supper at Mrs. Hind's in the evening. Sun. Mar. 19th/11

Met Dulcie & Gordon Runkle. She asked me to her place for Monday eve. Sat. May 6th/11

Anniversary of the late Queen Victoria's birth. Lovely day. Juke's Launch party. Spent the day at Brighton Beach. Muriel Merritt, Dulcie, Miss Hall, Sue, Miss Jukes, Harold, Mr. Jukes, Eddy M. his wife.
Wed. May 24th/11

Dulcie & Brett came in. Thurs. June 1st/11

Walked to the Bay with E.B. Band Concert. 10:30 met Dulcie & Naylor. Walked home with Naylor.
Tue. June 6th/11

Theatre Party "Prisoner of Zenda". Dulcie, Miss Fraser, Miss Biggs, Egerton, Gardiner, Lamont, Hesketh Biggs.
Fri. June 23rd/11

Raining. Played Bridge at the Smith's. Dulcie, Chrissie, Rita, Hedley. We won 396-132. Monday June 26th/11

Took Dulcie to the Theatre to see "Cameo Kirby".
Rotten. Thurs. July 13th/11

6 P.M. Went rowing with Dick Bennet. Pair oared skiff. Walked home with Dulcie. Fri. Aug. 25th/11

Dulcie's walking party. Beautiful clear night. Dulcie, Douglas, Sue, Gordon Runkle, Chrissie Smith, MacGee, Margot Whitney, Ted Mathews, Jean McGillivray, myself. Supper at the Hornby's afterwards.
Tue. Oct. 10th/11

Clare Battle's name also appeared often in Wallace's 1911 diary. The year began with Wallace describing Clare fondly.

~

Visited the Industrial School with Clare and took her to tea at the Ritz. She is a dear girl. Mon. Jan. 2nd/11

4:30 Tea with Clare & Arthur. Sat. 14th/11

Took Clare to Dance in aid of Seaman's Institute. Edith Townley, Miss Ruddick were there. Afterwards went to the club dance. Jan. 16th/11

Walked home with Clare at noon. Wed. Jan. 25th/11

Dance at North Vancouver Badminton Club. Took Clare. Got home 3:30 A.M. Very jolly. Fri. Jan. 27th/11

Tea at Mrs. Hinds with Clare. Sun. Jan. 29th/11

4:30 P.M. Called on Mrs. Oliphant Bell at the Richmond with Clare. Met Miss Gerry-Smith. Sat. Feb. 11th/11

~

In February, Clare left Vancouver to take a job in Kamloops. Her departure seemed to have been unexpected, at least by Wallace. On January 24, he had declared confidently in his diary that she would accompany him to a Madame Calvé concert on February 20. By then, however, Clare had packed and was on her way. Wallace's diary entry that day simply stated: *"Clare B. left for Kamloops at 9:00 A.M."* Subsequent entries showed that he and

Clare stayed in touch, but how often? Typically, Wallace provided few details, but he did save a clipping about her departure.

LOCAL JOURNALIST LEAVES

Miss Clare Battle, who for some years past has been engaged in journalistic work in Vancouver, left for Kamloops yesterday. Miss Battle has filled the office of secretary to the Vancouver branch of the Canadian Woman's Press Club, and prior to her departure that society presented her with a handsome gift, which was accompanied by the good wishes of all the members. Vancouver readers will no doubt continue to see articles from Miss Battle's pen.

Vancouver World account of Clare Battle's departure

After two and a half months in Kamloops, Clare returned to Vancouver, but Wallace did not note seeing her until a week later. Was this the first time he had spoken to her since her return? Her name continued to be prominent in Wallace's diary for a few months. They talked by telephone, went for walks, joined friends for cards, and played tennis. Sometimes Wallace noted that Clare was going out of town, likely on a journalistic assignment. On September 14, he wrote in his diary: *"Clare Battle spent the evening at our place. Brett Barwick & Robertson came in — played Bridge."* After that, there was no further mention of her this year.

Was Wallace afraid that he was getting too deeply involved with Clare? Or was it Clare's concern that they were seeing too much of each other? And what about Dulcie? Whatever the nature of Wallace's relationships with Dulcie and Clare, he also saw a lot of Eugenie

Brünn. She was a mystery woman. Although Wallace recorded that her address was 1872 Georgia, just seven blocks west of the Chambers residence, he did not mention her family connections or what, if anything, she did for a living. Throughout the year, Wallace noted that they went to many cultural functions together. He saw her usually at least once or twice a week, especially in the summer when they went walking or canoeing. The frequency of his outings with her, and the fact that they wrote each other letters even though they saw so much of each other, suggested a somewhat more than amiable relationship. Again, Wallace's diary provided few details other than where they went.

~

Took Eugenie to the Roller Rink. She's awfully nice.
Tuesday Jan. 31/11

Last of the Club dances. Very jolly — got home 2 A.M.
Lent begins tomorrow. Eugenie looked very well.
Feb. 28th/11

Wrote to E.B. Wed. Mar. 8th/11

Walked to the Bay with Eugenie. Wed. June 21st/11

8:30 Canoeing with Eugenie. Fri. July 7th/11

7 P.M. Paddling with E.B. Sun. July 9th/11

8:30 Took E.B. to hear Ellery's Band. Wed. Aug. 2nd/11

8 P.M. E.B. & I went out in the canoe. Listened to the
band playing on U.S. "West Virginia" Fri. Aug. 4th/11

Had card from Eugenie from Matsqui.
Thurs. Aug. 24th/11

~

But perhaps Wallace was troubled by his relationship with Eugenie. He had been spending an inordinate amount of time with her. And his letter-writing exchange with Cecie had been heating up. Wallace took Eugenie for a walk on September 26, the day after receiving a letter from Cecie, then visited Eugenie at her home a few days later. The next day, after going to church, he underlined *"Made resolution"* in his diary. Was this to terminate, or at least cool, his relationship with Eugenie?

Wallace may have discovered that relationships were hard to break up. What about Eugenie's feelings? She phoned him the following Thursday, and the next night he took her to the theatre. On October 20, Wallace confessed that he had broken his resolution, but promised to renew it. His diary mentioned no more of Eugenie until late December.

~

E. rang up. Thurs. Oct. 5th/11

Took E.B. to theatre. Fri. Oct. 6th/11

Broke resolution made Oct. 1st. Resolved again!! This time for good. Fri. Oct. 20th/11

Went with E.B. to hear the "Messiah" in St. John's Church. They sang it very well. Thurs. Dec. 28/11

~

Cecie

Wallace's first 1911 notation about Cecie was on March 1, when he received a letter which must have had some appealing contents. His diary noted that she was "a dear girl" and that he would like $10,000 to visit her! Although at first weeks passed before he replied to her letters, gradually he began to reply very quickly. And her two September letters interested him so much that he underlined them in his diary.

~

Had letter from Cecie. Tue. Sept. 19th/11

Had letter from Cecie acknowledging photos, etc. Monday Sept. 25th/11

~

But alas! After receiving one letter from Cecie in October, weeks went by with no word! Not even at Christmas! Wallace sent her three dozen carnations and mailed a Christmas letter, and was disappointed not to hear from her on Christmas Day. On December 27, he finally received a cablegram! New Year's Eve, while others were loudly celebrating, Wallace walked alone, thinking of Cecie. Was it possible he could be in love with a girl he had not seen since 1905?

~

7:30 St. John's Church. Good sermon by Mr. Pidgeon on "Resolutions". 12 P.M. Lovely clear frosty night. The New Year ushered in with tooting of horns,

*whistles blowing, bells ringing, etc. Went for a walk
by myself at midnight — thinking about Cecie.
Sun. Dec. 31st/11*

~

Military Activities

Wallace was becoming more involved in military activities,
and appeared to enjoy them, whether drilling or appearing
on dress parade or being inspected. Being in the military
also offered more opportunities for dances! In the spring,
Wallace began a series of evening classes — Non Cours[3]
or NCO (Non-Commissioned Officer) training courses
leading up to his becoming a sergeant in D Company,
72nd Canadian Scottish Highlanders.

~

*Teddy Palmer & I went down to the Drill Hall. Billy
Hunt & Cecie Bremer & Bresscy were there. Bernard
Formley enlisted in the 72nd Highlanders.
Wed. Feb. 15th/11*

*7 P.M. Non Cours. 72nd Highlander's class. First
experience at drilling a squad. Non Cours Class.
Came off pretty well. Mon. April 3rd/11*

*7 P.M. Appointed Sergeant 72nd Highlanders by
Capt. Godson, Adjt. Tue. Apr. 18th/11*

*7:45 P.M. A.B. & D. Co's Drill at the Armouries.
I am Sergeant of #2 Section D Company.
Tuesday May 2nd/11*

72nd Highlanders & 6th D.C.O.R. Officers Ball, also officers of H.M.C.S. Rainbow. Enjoyed the dance very much. Met Mrs. Herchmer, wife of Col. Herchmer. Wed. May 10th/11

⌒

The day after his twenty-fifth birthday, Wallace received his uniform. He obviously relished opportunities for wearing the kilt.

HIGHLANDERS INSPECTED
The crowds who turned out on Saturday afternoon to witness the first annual parade of the 72nd High-landers on Cambie Street grounds were loud in their praises on the good showing made by the men. After the inspection Lieut.-Col. R.G. Edwards Leckie, the officer com-manding, was the recipient of many compliments on the appearance the regiment made. Col. Wadmore con-gratulated the officers commanding, and the various company officers on bringing the regiment to such a high state of efficiency in so short a time, and expressed himself as well satisfied.

Clipping from *Vancouver World,* Aug. 12, 1911

⌒

72nd Highlanders on parade, 1911
(Photo from Vancouver Public Library Collection #9541)

Drill. Got my uniform. Very swagger. Wed. May 31st/11

8:45 Paraded for Company Drill at armouries for the first time in KILTS. Hoot Mon! Wed. June 7th/11

Went out to the Rifle Ranges at Richmond for the first time. Made 2 Bulls eyes at 500 yards. Sat. June 17th/11

First Full Dress Battalion parade. Wed. June 21st/11

Coronation Day. King George V England crowned. 72nd Highlanders in the Parade. Thurs. June 22nd/11

72nd Highlanders Inspection by D.O.C. Col. Wadmore Sat. Aug. 12th/11.

9 A.M. 40 men of the 72nd Highlanders formed guard of Honour to Admiral Togo of the Japanese fleet. Col. Wadmore complimented us on our appearance. Admiral Togo is one of the greatest commanders of the world. Sun. Aug. 27th/11

～

One other benefit of military activities? As far as Wallace was concerned, there were new opportunities for physical activities.

～

Went to the Highland sports at Brockton Point with Morrison. Our company won the Tug of War. Sat. July 29th/11

72nd Highlanders Football Club organized. Tue. Aug. 22nd/11

Playing Soccer for 72nd Highlanders.
Wed. Aug. 30th/11

8 P.M. Sergeants of the 72nd Regiment meeting re
Garrison Sports on the 16th. Thurs. Sept. 7th/11

Rowing Club 7:15 A.M. Raining. Our Crew
representing 72nd Highlanders: Cap't Markham,
F Co'y, Stroke; Myself, D Co'y, #3; Sgt. Kinred, F Co'y,
#2; Corp'l McRoberts, F Co'y, Bow. Fri. Sept. 8th/11

Our crew was defeated by Bank of Commerce crew.
Kennedy of Victoria won the Singles from Bonnie
Townley. Bank of Montreal won Murray Cup.
Sat. Sept 9th/11

Worked at office till 4 P.M. Football match 72nd
defeated by St. Andrews 6-0. First league game.
Sat. Sept. 30th/11

Hockey match, our team 72nd vs Vanc. at Brockton
Pt. Lieut. Bell Irving, Lieut. Kemp, Capt. Rae, Lc.
Corp. Watt, Corp. Watson, Sgt. Chambers, Lieut.
Oliphant, Sgt. Macrae. We were defeated 4-0.
Sat. Nov. 18th/11

～

While military activities and friendships provided new opportunities for physical and social activities, Wallace at the same time found that he needed to apply himself to achieve his certificate as a sergeant. While he might meet new bridge companions such as Dr. Gillies,[4] he would also sometimes have to turn down a social invitation, such as one from Chrissie Marshall-Smith in early December.

His classes included lectures on Military Law, the Parts of a Rifle, Interior Economy & Duties, Martial Law, Military Tactics, Skirmishing, Outpost Duty, Brigade Advancing to Attack, and Musketry Regulations. Instructors were Colonel Arthur Youngman of Victoria, and Sergeant Instructor Coffin. By the end of the year, Wallace's preparations and tests were over, and he could celebrate at the Military Ball.

~

Will drill every night now for six weeks, School of Instruction. Will get certificate as Sgt when finished. Wed. Oct. 25th/11

Bridge at Dr. Gillies. Miss Leckie & Col. Leckie, 72nd Highlanders. Sat. Nov. 4th/11

Chrissie Smith's Bridge. Have to attend drill— so can't go, worse luck. Thurs. Dec. 7th/11

Final Exam Interior Economy & Duties. Supper Party afterwards — gave the instructors purses — speeches etc. songs till 1 A.M. Thurs. Dec. 14th/11

Military Ball in Lester Hall. Jolly Dance. The bright uniforms of the Highlanders & 6th D.C.O.R. looked awfully well. Met Miss Knoope & girl from Germany. Charming. Dec. 15th/11

Officers D Company: Montague Moore, Cap't.; R.O. Bell Irving, Lieut.; W.H. Kemp, Lieut.; J.D. Spence, Co. Serg't; M.R.J. Reid, Serg't; S.W.G. Chambers, Serg't; Brady, Serg't; Wrightson, Serg't. Dec. 31/11

~

Notes

1. Heath was a clerk in the Canadian Bank of Commerce, and lived at 745 Burrard Street, close to Alberni Avenue.

2. Col. Thomas Owen Townley was the first commander of the No. 5 Company, B.C. Battalion of Garrison Artillery. He was a barrister, a land registrar, and at the turn of the century, mayor of Vancouver. In 1911, he was the District Registrar of Titles, with an office in the court house. The family home was at 1125 Seaton Street. (For more information, see *The Greater Vancouver Book,* by Chuck Davis, editor-in-chief, Linkman Press, 15032-97th Avenue, Surrey, B.C., 1997.)

3. Wallace appears to have used the term "non cours" to mean "non-commissioned."

4. This was Dr. George Ernest Gillies, who later served overseas in Wallace's regiment. In 1911, Ernest Gillies was recorded as living in the same residence as his older brother, Dr. B.D. Gillies, at 1281 Broughton.

Chapter 6

~

1912

"Everything Is Rosy"

This was a year of several major changes for Wallace.
Early in the year, he became engaged to Cecie, the woman
he had corresponded with, but not seen, for seven years.
In the middle of the year, he not only received a promotion,
but also decided to buy a house. Throughout, he became
increasingly involved in his regiment's military activities.

Cecie

Wallace had spent New Year's Eve 1911 walking alone
and thinking of Cecie. That evening influenced all of
Wallace's activities in 1912. A letter he received from Cecie
in mid-January was the first from her in three months (if
he didn't count the cablegram she sent after Christmas
1911) and it was very welcome. A few days later, another
letter from Cecie arrived. Did she signal that her heart was
warm to Wallace? The letter had a stunning impact on
him. That very night Wallace walked through the frosty
night to post an important request.

~

*9 A.M. Got letter from C.E.F. Also picture called "Cold
Hands But a Warm Heart". Awfully pretty. 11 P.M.
Wrote to Cecie. The most important letter I ever
wrote!!! Walked down to Post Office at midnight to
post it. (Slight frost.) Thurs. Jan. 18/12.*

～

For more than a month, Wallace remained in suspense.
In February, after mailing her a birthday letter and book,
The Weaver of Dreams by Myrtle Reid, he received photos
of Cecie: *"The full length one is lovely — she is so
beautiful!"* One day after her birthday, he received the
message he was so eagerly awaiting: he and Cecie were
engaged! From that point on, his diary contained many
underlined words.

～

*Lovely bright day. Noon — got letter from Cecie. I am
engaged now — so everything is rosy.
Friday, Feb. 23rd/12*

*My thoughts are full of Cecilia these days. 9 P.M.
Wrote to Cecie in answer to her Tuesday important
one. Mon. Feb. 26th/12*

*Ordered 3 doz. roses to be sent to Cecie. Ordered
from Mrs. Prockter, Floral Hall, Brighton. Pd 12/-
Feb. 27th/12*

～

Like migratory birds, their letters and picture post cards
(P.P.C.) criss-crossed the ocean.[1] Wallace wrote to Cecie's

father in Bolivia, South America, formally asking for his consent to the engagement, and received a letter of congratulations from Cecie's brother, Connie. In the midst of a constant flow of gifts and love-letters, Wallace was generally in high spirits, although he admitted to feeling "down" one Saturday night. In mid-April, Cecie sent a message which caused him some anguish. What could it have been? Wallace offered no clue. Now his happiness hinged on what the mail brought.

~

Got a beautiful embroidered pyjama case from Cecie. Also Easter card. Wed. Apr. 3rd/12

Sent "Molly Make Believe" to Cecie. Letter from Cecie posted Mar. 20th. 9 P.M. Feel very "Blue" tonight. Sat. Apr. 6th/12

9 A.M. Letter from Cecie. 3 P.M. Got very <u>important</u> and <u>sad</u> letter from Cecie. I absolutely wept when I read it. 12 P.M. Went to bed feeling very miserable. April 15th/12

Felt <u>very</u> miserable all day — owing to what Cecie told me in her letter yesterday. Tue. Apr. 16th/12

Raining. No letter from Cecie this week — very disappointed. Sat. Apr. 27th/12

I was introduced to Cecie this day — no, it was 29th of May seven years ago. I never dreamed that I should ever be engaged to her. Mon. Apr. 29th/12

I am doing my best to live an upright, manly life and so become worthy of dear Cecie's love. What a wonderful thing <u>true love</u> is. Mon. May 6th/12

Worked all day. 6 P.M. Ordered some roses to be sent to Cecie. Sat. May 11th/12

Lovely warm day. Spent the day in the Garden, reading & thinking of Cecie. Sun. May 12th/12

This is my birthday, got a lovely pocket book & card from Cecie. Thurs. May 30th/12

These days are very happy ones — Cecie's letters are charming. She is the dearest girl in the world. My life would be so empty without her love. I only hope that my letters to her give her one half the happiness hers bring to me. Tue. June 4th/12

～

For the next three months, Wallace was troubled by letters from Cecie's "old friend," Harry Broadwood (H.B.). Whether Broadwood was a former boyfriend of Cecie or not, Wallace did not say, but Broadwood seemed intent on souring the Wallace-Cecie relationship. Where Broadwood lived was not clear, but his replies to letters suggested that it was not abroad. Perhaps in another location in Canada? Even as Wallace replied to Broadwood's letters, he reassured himself about Cecie by reading through all the letters he had received from her since 1905. Though he wanted to send her a ring of her favourite jewel, emerald, it was beyond his budget, and in June, he sent a seal ring instead.

～

9 A.M. Had letter from Harry Broadwood, an old friend of Cecie's. His letter worries me. 9:30 A.M. wrote to Cecie about Harry. Sat. June 8th/12

Spent the afternoon reading old letters, mostly Cecie's dating from Aug. 1905. Sun. June 9th/12

P.P.C. from Cecie. She is at Worthing, Eng. for the summer. Wrote to Harry Broadwood, replied to his letter. Tuesday June 11th/12

Bo't seal ring for Cecie with initial S.W.C. Size 6 — 14 Karat. Pd 6.50. Was talking to Ken Taylor today — he knows Harry Broadwood & his sister Dorothy. Wed. June 12th/12

Noon — letter from Cecie. Wrote to Mrs. Fernau. 9 P.M. Arthur & I walked to the Bay & thru the Park. Big surf running at the Bay. Evening star very bright. I wish Cecie were here. Fri. June 14th/12

Spent the evening reading and thinking of C.E.F. Sun. June 16th/12

Wrote to Cecie. 9 A.M. Letter from Cecie, also from Harry Broadwood. Mon. June 17th/12

4 P.M. Mailed ring to Cecie. Tue. June 18th/12

By Jove, this is going to be a glorious day — got a 32 page letter from Cecie — at 9 A.M. Fri. June 21st/12

Slight rain. Noon: Wrote to Cecie. 2:30 P.M. Had a letter from Cecie. The dear sweet girl sent me a lock of her hair. Thurs. June 27th/12

While Wallace received some approving messages from Cecie's family abroad, including a letter from her mother and her father's consent to their engagement, Broadwood continued to try to dampen Wallace's loving feelings for Cecie.

~

Had a nice letter from Cecie's cousin Vi Fernau written from her home in Casa Blanca Morocco congratulating me on my engagement.
Tue. July 2nd/12

Wrote to Miss V. Fernau. This day seven years ago Cecie & I went riding & walked up the mt. through lovely trees, back of the smelter at Frank. While we were walking, my horse "Donnybrook" went astray. Had a deuce of a time finding him. This was one of the pleasantest days of my life. Cecie was charming. Fri. July 12th/12

Thinking of Cecie all the time. Rec'd two books from Cecie "Pools of Silence" by De Vere Stackpole & book of "sayings" and verses compiled by herself. Letter from H. Broadwood. Thurs. July 18th/12

Wrote to Cecie. H.B.'s letters worry me. Sent Cecie Hat Pin 72nd Highlanders Button, also song Love's Coronation. Friday July 19th/12

~

Wallace wanted go to London, to talk Broadwood's letters over with Cecie in person, but it was beyond his budget.

~

Got Bible from Cecie today, also G.B. Shaw's book Man & Superman. Wed. July 24th/12

Had letter from H.B. — wrote to Cecie, short note about H.B. It worries me. Thursday July 25th/12

I am thinking of C.E.F. all the time. I think H.B. is a silly ass but I can tell by his letters that he has some good points. He is trying to embitter me against Cecie. Thurs. July 25/12

Posted letter to Cecie. 7:30 went to St. John's with Ian Gibson. Walked home (4 miles), took me one hour. Glorious night — enjoyed the walk very much — thinking of Cecie most of the time. Sunday July 28th/12

Thinking about going to London to see Cecie. Tue. July 30th/12

~

Broadwood's arguments seemed not to obliterate Wallace's ability to day-dream about Cecie. His day was made if he heard from her; not receiving a message caused him to pine.

~

3:30 went to the Park on my bike (five miles). Went out in canoe and read "Man the Superman" & listened to band concert, and thought of Cecie. Enjoyed the afternoon immensely. Sunday Aug. 4/12

No letter from C.E.F. this morning. Very disappointed. 11 A.M. Mailed Gertie's photo to Cecie. Lord! I hope Cecie's letter comes tomorrow. Monday Aug. 5/12

2 letters and P.P.C. from Cecie. 8 P.M. Wrote to C.E.F Tuesday Aug. 6/12

Lovely morning. Posted letter to Cecie written last night. Wed. Aug. 7/12

Had a peculiar dream of Cecie last night — thought her eyes turned blue. I kissed her too. It was so realistic that I've been in fine spirits all day. Friday Aug. 9/12

Wrote to Cecie today. Sent a snap of Vanc. In the evening I read a lot of old letters. Didn't go to church. Thinking of C.E.F. Sunday Aug. 11/12

Lovely day. I hope there will be a letter from Cecie tomorrow. Monday Aug. 12/12

Clear and warm. Note from Cecie this morning. Got a lovely long letter from Cecie this afternoon. 11 P.M. wrote to Cecie. Tuesday Aug. 13/12

∼

By the end of August, Broadwood's letters had begun to erode Wallace's confidence in Cecie. He often tried to reassure himself by rereading Cecie's letters. Throughout, his long-distance communication with Cecie continued, nurtured by their mutual appreciation of art, music, books, and all things beautiful. Finally, by early September, Wallace put his doubts to rest.

~

Had a note from H.B. today. 4 P.M. Wrote to H.B. Thursday Aug. 15/12

Letter from Cecie. Letter from H.B. today. Thursday Aug. 22/12

9 P.M. Reading Cecie's letters and thinking about her. Friday Aug. 23/12

3:30 Wrote to Cecie. In the evening got a pretty little picture from Cecie by McWirster. It is her favourite picture in the Tate Gallery. Saturday Aug. 24/12

5 P.M. Posted letter to Cecie. 6 P.M. Letter from Cecie in answer to mine about H.B. It hurt and puzzled me. Thursday Aug. 29/12

8:30 Read a lot of Cecie's letters to reassure myself of her love. I cannot doubt her letters. Friday Aug. 30/12

Raining heavily. Stayed at home all day reading "Emerson's Essays", "Ingoldsby Legends", Cecilia's letters, "Pleas for Faith", and Bible. Sunday Sept. 1/12

7:30 Spent the evening reading, and writing to Cecie. Monday Sept. 2/12 Labour Day

6 P.M. 3 letters from Cecie. No longer any doubt about her love. Tuesday Sept. 3/12

∽

Although Harry Broadwood persisted with his interfering letters, Wallace no longer seemed troubled by them. By mid-October, Wallace had decided that Broadwood was "of unsound mind," and never mentioned him again this year.

∽

Got 2 books from Cecie — "Clementina" & "Diana Tempest". Fine bright evening, slightly frosty. Letter from Cecie enclosing 3 of H.B. Tuesday Sept 24/12

Had letter from H.B. Friday Sept. 27/12

Answered H.B.'s letter. Monday Sept. 30/12

3 <u>charming</u> letters from Cecie today. She writes beautiful letters and they do me so much good. I wish I were worthy of her affection. I wish I could afford to buy her a nice necklace or an Emerald & Diamond ring. Wed. Oct. 2/12

<u>Wrote to Cecie.</u> Saturday Oct. 5/12

Letter from H.B. Tuesday Oct. 8/12

Had 2 books from Cecie today, "The Princess Passes", "The Lightening Conductor" — Williamson. Thursday Oct. 10/12

Letter from H.B. Judging from his letters I would say he is of unsound mind. Mon. Oct. 14/12

~

Throughout the fall, Wallace sent or received letters and post cards most days, culminating in flowers, music, and a pendant for Cecie at Christmas.

~

Cloudy. 2 letters & several P.P.C. from Cecie yesterday. Ordered 2 doz. carnations to be sent to Cecie from Floral Hall, Brighton. 10 P.M. Wrote to Cecie. Wed. Nov. 6/12

Bo't pendant for Cecie $40.00 — X'mas present. Friday Nov. 22/12

I think I will send Mrs. Fernau some chrysanthemums for X'mas and roses to Cecie. Tuesday Nov. 26/12

11 A.M. Have just received a sweet letter from Cecilia. She is a darling girl — and I love her — would give almost anything to talk to her now. Thursday Nov. 28/12

Bought Schubert's Impromptu in B Flat for Gertie, as Cecie is learning it & I like to be familiar with the pieces she plays. Friday Nov. 29/12

Had a delightful dream last night — thought I was having dinner with Cecie. Fully expected letter from Cecie today — but was disappointed. Wednesday Dec. 11th/12

Very jolly Xmas, but I wish Cecie's letter had come today. I would have been happier. Cecie was in my thoughts all day. Wednesday Dec. 25/12

~

Family

Now that Sue was engaged to Fred Townley (F.L.T.),[2] he was an even more frequent visitor at the Chambers home. Although he was a chum of Wallace, both had to fulfil the obligations that the era demanded of gentlemen — since Sue's father was deceased, Wallace, her older brother, was the one who would give Fred consent to marry Sue. In addition to recording his own correspondence with Cecie and her family after their engagement, Wallace now recorded the enfolding of Sue and Fred into each other's families.

~

F.L.T. had a talk with me about his engagement to Sue. He asked my permission, which I granted. Wed. Feb. 7th/12

Sue and I are lunching together every day now at the Wedgewood. It is very pleasant. This is F.L.T's birthday (25). Wed. July 17th/12

F.L.T. called. Sue at Townley's for dinner. Came home at 11 P.M. Tue. July 30th/12

Sue went out on the Townley's boat today. Sunday Aug. 4/12

Sue at Townley's for dinner. Monday Aug. 26/12

*Sue got a lovely diamond hoop ring from F.L.T.
today. Wed. Sept. 25/12*

*8:30 P.M. F.L.T. came out. Brought roses and violets
for Sue. Wed. Nov. 27/12*

~

Gertie this year would be twenty-two, but Wallace and
Maude, the older brother and sister, were still protective.
During many of her outings, Gertie was chaperoned by
her brother or a sister or friend of the family. Throughout
the winter and spring, however, Wallace's diary recorded
that Gertie and Wilfred Middleton (Middy) were often at
the same event, and Middleton visited the Chambers home
frequently. (As described by Wallace in 1911, Middleton
was the bank accountant who played the piano well.) In
late April, Wallace used cryptic brackets to record in his
diary that Gertie was engaged to Middy. In August, Wallace
mailed a photo of Gertie to Mrs. Middleton, but this was
his last reference to the engagement or to Wilfred
Middleton.[3]

~

*Gertie went to dance in North Vancouver with Mrs.
Cosgrove. Wed. Jan. 3rd/12*

*Accepted Mrs. Chappelle's invitation for Thursday
B.C. Golf Club Ball tonight. Gertie is going with
Meredith. Mrs. Chappelle chaperone. Fri. Jan. 19th/12*

*Lovely spring day. Middy came in for tea.
Sun. Jan. 21/12*

7:30 P.M. Middy came up. Saturday Jan. 27th.

Gertie & Mac went to Orpheum. Mon. Jan. 29th/12

7 P.M. dinner at the Dunsmuir. Connie, Middy, Sue, Maude, Gertie & I. Sunday February 11th/12

8 P.M. Sue & Gertie have gone to a dance in North Vanc. Wed. Feb. 14th/12

Gertie, Middy went to Hockey Match. Tuesday March 12th/12

8:30 Mac & Gerald, Noel Hunt, Middy & Arthur in for the evening. Sat. Mar. 16th/12

7 P.M. Middy in for Dinner. Fri. Mar 22nd/12

8:30 Middy, Mac & Gerald came in. Sun. Mar. 24th/12

(Gertie & Middy are engaged). Sun. Apr. 28th/12

Mailed photo of Gertie to Mrs. Middleton, 11 Deanville Rd., Clapham Park, London, Eng. Thursday Aug. 8/12

~

In the fall, Gertie underwent surgery for varicose veins. She was in the care of Dr. B.D. Gillies, one of the physicians who had treated Mary in her final illness. During Gertie's convalescence, Wallace and her sisters and friends typically rallied around, visiting her with flowers and gifts.

~

Sunny day. Gertie is going to Burrard Sanitarium this evening to undergo operation. Dr. B.D. Gillies will operate. She will be in bed for a month or six weeks — poor girl. Thursday Sept. 5/12

Raining. Called at Burrard Sanitarium, Georgia St., to see Gertie. The operation was quite successful. She was under Ether for three hours. Poor girl is very weak. She has a good special nurse, Miss Leitch. 9:30 Called again. Gertie is much brighter. Friday Sept. 6/12

Raining. 10 A.M. Went to see Gertie. Took some Belfast Ginger Ale which the Dr. says she might have. Saturday Sept. 7/12

Called to see Gertie, took some grapes for her. She is much brighter today. Monday Sept. 9/12

Called to see Gertie. She is feeling better today. Miss Hornby, Miss Cuthbertson & Sue were there. She had lots of lovely flowers. Thurs. Sept. 12/12

Lovely day. Gertie came home today from hospital. Thursday Sept. 19/12

~

Wallace did not often mention his sister, Edith, or his niece, Phyllis, in his diary. His most frequent reference was to Edith's husband, Arthur Blanchet, who accompanied him on many outings. It was likely that sometimes Edith and Phyllis went along, too. Wallace recorded that he and Arthur had taken Phyllis canoeing in August, and that he had gone to the beach and built sand castles with Phyllis on "a lovely bright day" in October. Wallace also noted that he took Edith to several cultural events throughout the year.

Work

A few months after his third year with Evans, Coleman & Evans (E.C. & E.), Wallace received another promotion, and was now in charge of the office. His brother-in-law, Arthur Blanchet (A.L.B.), started work as an accountant with the firm, but found a more suitable job a few months later, with the help of family connections. In the fall, Wallace briefly considered other employment opportunities, but apparently decided to stay with E.C. & E. By Christmas, Wallace was welcoming a raise and a turkey for the family.

~

3 years today since I started with Evans Coleman & Evans. Thurs. Feb. 15/12

I have been promoted & am now in charge of office at 407 Granville. Saturday June 1st/12

A.L.B. started with E.C.& E. today. Wed. Mar. 27th/12

Arthur resigned position today with E.C. & E., has good position with Dom. Trust Co. offered him through my uncle, G.F. Gibson. Thursday Oct. 31/12

Met Rob't Mungall. We are thinking of going into business — mfgers agents, brokers etc. Thurs. Sept. 26/12

Mr. Thomson Timm approached me today with an offer of a position at $150.00 per month as manager

*of Lumber Mill on Vancouver Island. I am to give him
an answer in a few days. Friday Oct. 4/12*

*Mr. Russell has given me an increase in salary of
10.00 per month. Also a turkey from the firm.
Dec. 23/12*

~

Real Estate Investments

On May 31, having just turned twenty-six, Wallace
heard that the rent for the house at 1155 Georgia Street
would be raised to $60 per month. He and his sisters
were faced with a decision: rent or buy? Susan would be
married soon, and perhaps Gertie. Maude was still
working for a legal firm. The economy continued to be
brisk, and Wallace's job seemed promising. Within ten
days he declared in his diary that he had bought a six-
room house at 2532 Balaclava Road for $4,800. The down
payment was $200 and a $900 equity in a West Broadway
lot between Vine and Balsam which he and his sister,
Maude, had purchased in October 1909.

From Wallace's diary, it was not clear whether Maude
was participating in the ownership of the new home.
However, the mathematics suggested that she may have
been. In addition to the $200 down payment and the $900
equity, Wallace was assuming a $2,500 mortgage over a
period of two years: $200 + $900 + $2,500 = $3,600. The
other $1,200 of the purchase was not accounted for. Did
Maude contribute the balance? Wallace did not say. In
August, Wallace still owned his lot in Grandview, at
Garden and Tenth Avenue, when Arthur sold his lot in the
same neighbourhood to his brother, Guy Blanchet, for $700.

~

Rec'd notice that rent wd be raised to 60.00 per month on July 10th. Consequently am on the lookout for another house. Fri. May 31st/12.

Bo't House Lot today from Vernon Bros. Lot D re sub of lots 28 & 29 B 33, D.L. 192 (Balaclava Rd near 10th Ave) 6 rooms. 4800.00. 900.00 equity in Broadway lot & 200 as first payment— assume 2500 mortgage a 8%, bal. over 2 years at 7%. Mon. June 10th/12

Got Cheque from Can. Life Ass. 195.00 loan on my policy, int. 5 1/2 %. this is to help make the first payment on the house I bought. Mon. June 17th/12

Occupied new house 2532 Balaclava Road today— Kitsilano. Moving seems to be a stupendous undertaking before one starts, but after one has "buckled to" and it is finished, it doesn't appear to be much of a job. Tue. July 9th/12

# of application to register property on Balaclava Road is #65887. Tuesday Aug. 13/12

Guy & I went to look at my lot in Grandview. He is buying Arthur's lot west to mine for $700.00 cash. Wed. August 28/12

~

Church

Even though his new home was four miles away, and he sometimes tried another church closer by, Wallace remained loyal to St. John's Church. As in previous years, his diary usually recorded what the music was like and what he thought of the sermon.

～

7:30 P.M. Went to St. John's Church with Mac. Miss Eileen McGuire sang — very good voice. Sun. Jan. 14th/12

7:30 went to St. John's Church. Miss McGuire sang "Abide with Me". She has a lovely rich contralto voice. Sun. Jan. 21/12

7:30 St. John's Church. Rev. Dr. McKay preached. Middy, Gertie, & Sue went to Christ Church. Sunday Feb. 18th/12

72nd Highlander's Church parade to St. John's. Rev. John McKay the Chaplain preached. Sun. Mar. 31st/12

Went to St. John's Church. Good sermon by Rev. Mr. Forrest — "Honour thy Father, thy Mother, that thy days may be long in the land the Lord thy God giveth thee." Sun. July 7th/12

Went to hear Rev. Peter Wright preach his farewell sermon — very good. Sunday Sept. 22/12

Rain. Stayed in the house all day reading. 7:30 walked to St. John's & walked home again afterwards (4 miles each way). Sun. Sept. 29/12

7:30 Maude, Gertie & I went to St. John's Anniversary Services. Sun. Nov. 3/12

*7 P.M. Anniversary Banquet at St. John's Church.
MacArthur and I went together. Friday Nov. 8/12*

*7:30 St. John's with Maude. Good sermon by Dr.
McQueen. Mrs. Cave, Miss McGuire & Mrs Schultz
sang a trio beautifully. Sunday Nov. 10/12*

*2 P.M. Church Parade to Mt. Pleasant Church. The
cadets came with us. It was their initial parade.
Owing to pouring rain, the parade was postponed.
7:30 St. John's Church. Sunday Dec. 1/12*

*2:30: 5 mile walk to Point Grey. 7:30 St. John's
Church Christmas Service. Walked home with Ian &
Harold & Arthur. Sun. Dec. 22/12*

～

Outdoors

The extra distance from his new home to work, church,
and other activities made Wallace even more of a walker,
and biking the twenty minutes to and from work provided
welcome exercise for his energetic body. As usual, he also
enjoyed several sea adventures and a variety of other
outings and sports such as ice hockey and sculling. This
year, Wallace's field hockey team, the 72nd Highlanders,
was consistently trounced by its opponents, but his
sculling team did well at the spring regatta, beating two
other crews before going down to defeat.

～

*3 P.M. Played Field Hockey at North Vanc. They beat
us 7-1. Saturday January 27th/12*

3 P.M. Played Field Hockey 72nd vs Vanc. We lost. Sat. Feb. 10th/12

3 P.M. Field Hockey. Highlanders vs Victoria. They defeated us 4-0. Sat. Feb. 17th/12

3:30 Hockey Match. North Vanc. vs Highlanders. N.V. won 4-0. Had photo of teams taken. Sat. Mar. 16th/12

3:30 Went for walk with Arthur in Stanley Park. Sat. Mar. 23rd/12

Worked till 4 P.M. 4:30, went sculling. Sat. Apr. 13th/12

Had my first practice in a "four" for this season. Regatta next Saturday. Our crew: Owen Sawers stroke, myself # 3, E.G. Kerr # 2, Norman Sawers, Bow. Mon. Apr. 22nd/12

Beautiful clear day. 6 P.M. went for a row with Dr. Minogue Stroke, Myself # 3, Chaffey # 2, Munro. Wed. Apr. 24th/12

3 P.M. Spring Regatta. Our crew N.C. Sawers Stroke, Ken Taylor #2, myself # 3, Sherwood Bow. We beat Bk. of Hamilton crew easily. We beat Victoria by 1/2 a length. In the final McGachen's crew beat us by half length. Sat. Apr. 27th/12

72nd Regiment Field day at Kerrisdale. Got very sun burned. Returned 5 P.M. Sun. May 5th/12

~

Wallace had some pleasant outings as crew on friends' sail boats. For the May 24 week-end, he was a guest of Gordon Farrell for a three-day cruise with seven persons aboard. After overnighting at Nanaimo, they visited Buccaneer Bay and Pender Harbour before returning. Another week-end outing — a race — with Gordon Runkle on the "Canuck" in June unfortunately had to be abandoned when another crew member became ill. A third outing Wallace recorded was a July day's sailing with Robertson and friends on the yacht "Kehloke."

~

Empire day. Clear & warm. 9:30 A.M. Left on the Shieleena in race to Nanaimo — on board were Gordon, Kathleen, & Nora Farrell, Mrs. Brooke, Margot Whitney, Mr. Robbins & I. Went across in 3½ hours. Stayed there overnight. Friday May 24th/12

Misty, slight rain. Sailed for Buccaneer Bay. Mr. Brooke came aboard from the Commodore's yacht the "Aquilla". 3 P.M. Sailed for Pender Harbour. Sat. May 25th/12

Sailed for home today, arrived 7 P.M. after a glorious 3 day cruise. Sun. May 26th/12

1:30 P.M. Left on the yacht "Canuck" entered for race to White Rocks & back, we will sail all night & return tomorrow evening. Not much wind. 12 P.M. Still calm. 3 A.M. Wind freshening. 4 A.M. Good breeze. Sat. June 22nd/12

It got pretty rough. Conway-Miles got so ill we had to discontinue the race & take shelter in Howe Sound.

The trip was glorious. We all got very sunburned.
Sun. June 23rd/12

Rode in to office on my bike, took me 20 minutes,
pretty warm work too. Going sailing with Robertson
on Sunday. Friday July 19th/12

10 A.M. Went sailing on the "Kehloke" — Mr. Gee,
Mr. Brown, Robertson, Daniels, H.G. Watt. Miss
MacDonald, Joan Butler. Spent a very pleasant day.
Had lunch at Horseshoe Bay. Got home 9 P.M.
Sun. July 21st/12

~

This year the canoe was relatively neglected, or at least
not mentioned often. In August, Wallace and his brother-
in-law, Arthur, enjoyed a five-hour hike and a few weeks
later found them on another long walk in North Vancouver.
Wallace also often explored alone.

~

Cool & cloudy. Rode around Stanley Park on my
bike. Stopped to see a Cricket Match & Tennis at
Brockton Point. Also watched the Caledonian Sports
for half an hour. The ride through the park I enjoyed
very much. Saturday Aug. 3/12

Cloudy, rather sultry. 2:30 Arthur & I walked out to
Pt. Grey, branched off Alma Rd. at 12th Ave. & went
through timber in a south-westerly direction. After
about two hours walk through timber & occasional
open space we got to Marine Drive. We got a superb
view of the Gulf from the point. Walked home along

Marine Drive reaching there 7:30. Enjoyed this afternoon very much. Sunday Aug. 18/12

Worked at home in A.M. 2:45 Went for long walk over Shaughnessy Heights & over Little Mountain to S. Vanc. Monday Sept. 2/12, Labour Day

Lovely day. 3 P.M. Hockey match 72nd vs Burnaby. I missed the tram — so Arthur & I went to No. Vanc. & walked to Hollyburn — delightful path through the woods (4 miles). Came home from Hollyburn in launch — tea at Spencer's. Cinema afterwards. Saturday Sept. 28/12

Got up 8:45. Lovely morning. Went along to the Lucas-Hunts — we were going for a long walk, but they couldn't go, so I came home. Walked out to Eburne through Pt. Grey — some lovely homes there along Marine Drive. The colouring of the woods is exquisite. Fine view of the mouth of the Fraser and the Gulf. Sunday Oct. 20/12

~

Cultural Activities

In 1912, Wallace's cultural activities seemed to be somewhat reduced from other years. Was his spare time more and more taken up with Cecie and military activities? Or was he less able to afford cultural events now that he owned a house? In any case, as an engaged man, he was more likely than in previous years to be accompanied by family or male friends.

~

*D.L. Pachmann the great pianist at the Opera House.
January 1st/12*

*8:30 Theatre. C. James Bancroft in "The Private
Secretary". Mon. Jan. 22nd/12*

*Took Maude to see Forbes Robertson in his play "The
Passing of the Third Floor Back" Very fine play —
with good moral. Thurs. Jan. 25th/12*

*8:30 P.M. Gerald Heath brought his gramophone to
our house. Fred & Mac came in. We listened to
Kreisler, Mischa Elman, Melba, Tetrazzini, Calvé,
Nordica, Caruso. Sat. Feb. 17th/12*

~

Whether or not for financial reasons, Wallace
mentioned more lectures and amateur plays in his cultural
experience this year. Whether sisters Gertie and Maude
were interested in the science of bridge building he didn't
say!

~

*8:30 Took Gertie & Maude to Lecture on the Science
of Bridge Building. Sir Chas. Tupper, Chairman,
G.R.G. Conway lectured. Archeological Society.
Friday, Feb. 23rd/12*

*Took Maude & Gertie to the "Musical Ride" at the
Horse Show. Thurs. Feb. 29th/12*

*4 P.M. Rehearsal of Julius Caesar at Opera house —
with Mantell Company. Thursday March 7th/12*

Dr. Wilfred Grenfell Lecture. Very interesting. He has a beautiful character. Mon. Mar. 4th/12

Went with Oliphant to see the Gondoliers (amateur). Misses Ella Walker, Eileen McGuire, Babs McPherson, Jean McDonald — all very good. Geo. Chaffey & Hy Chrimes & E.K. Ricketts were good. Tuesday April 9th/12

Arthur & I went to see Wm. Faversham in the "Faun". It's very good and the acting splendid. The play shows how shallow & insincere is the modern society life. Thurs. May 2nd/12

Took Maude & Edith to see the "Pink Lady" at the Opera House. Music good. It was very funny. Song hits: "Girl by the Saskatchewan", "Beautiful Lady". Thursday May 16th/12

8:30 P.M. Took Edith to concert in Pender Hall. Conrad White has splendid baritone voice. He sang Oh Star of Eve. June 7th/12

8:30 P.M. Saw a third rate thing called "Vanity Isle". Saturday Aug. 31/12

Fine & clear. Last night Robertson brought a friend of his to our house, Von Gelden. He is a clerk in the Bk of Commerce — cultured & plays the piano very well. He played the Venetian Boat songs that Cecie likes & I thought of her all the time. Monday Sept. 23/12

8 P.M. went to Armouries, afterwards to cine & saw Sarah Bernhardt in La Tosca. Friday Oct. 25/12

~

Social Activities

When Wallace became committed to faraway Cecie, he made a resolution, it seemed, to cut off his relationship with Eugenie. Although he recorded that he took her skating in January, Eugenie was hardly mentioned in his 1912 diary. Now, to dances, he escorted his sisters, or went with a group of friends, including Connie Fernau, Cecie's brother.

~

6 P.M. Took Sue to Hockey match V.R.C. vs V.A.C. VAC won 6-1. Sat. Jan. 20th/12

9 P.M. Ladies Hockey Club Ball. Sue came with me. C. Fernau came as well. Very jolly. Sat. Feb. 10th/12

72nd Highlanders Officers Ball. Very swagger. Fri. Feb. 16th/12

Charity Ball — Victorian Order of Nurses — Lester Hall. Fred & Edith Townley and Frank Tupper went. I took Sue. It was too crowded for pleasure. Tue. Feb. 20th/12

7 P.M. Mrs. Sherrin of Souris had dinner with us. 9:00 P.M. Dr. Sherrin called. Dulcie rang up and congratulated me on my engagement. She was the first. No, Peggy Hunt was the first. Sat. Feb. 24th/12

4 P.M. Called on Mrs. Campbell-Chappell. 9 P.M. Sue and I went to supper at Colonel Townley's. They have a lovely house and supper was served beautifully. Sun. Feb. 25th/12

Bridge at Mrs. Hornby's. Madge MacFarlane, Nora Farrell, Chrissie Smith, Dulcie, Ted Matthews, Gordon Runkle, Wykham. Wed. Mar. 6th/12

~

This year, Wallace spent more time with his male friends, with whom he played cards, attended events, went for walks or shared meals. Whether dining at home or out, Wallace appreciated eating good food[4] in the company of friends — *"Had two chickens"; "Good supper"; "Had ice cream on the verandah."*

~

Ian Gibson & Arthur in for the evening. Had two chickens from Orine's ranch. Sun. Mar. 17th/12

Government House Ball in Victoria on the 18th. Letter. Rec'd invitation from Connie F. Letter from Connie S. 8:30. Mon. Apr. 8th/12

Lovely bright day. Connie met me, went to his rooms and to dinner. 9 P.M. Went up to Government house. Had a very good time — although the Ball Room was awfully crowded (1200 people). Good supper. Got home 4 A.M. Thurs. Apr. 18th/12

3:30 Called at Mrs. Hornby's as I was passing. Had ice cream on the verandah. 7 P.M. Had dinner at the "Carleton" with Mr. Sharpe & Miss Phyllis. Wed. July 10th/12

9 P.M. Brett Barwick & Gordon Runkle came out, also Guy & Arthur. We played "Rum". Thursday Aug. 29/12

Still fine. Chilly evenings. 1 P.M. Had lunch with Arthur & Percy McLean. 8:30 Walked to Strathcona going out Trafalgar Rd. Called in to see the Leighton Reids. Wed. Sept. 25/12

Gerald Heath & Percy McLean spent the evening at the house. We played "Rum". Wed. Oct. 9/12

H. & Ian Gibson spent the evening at the house, played Whist. Beatrice Westwood called this afternoon. Friday Oct. 11/12

~

Wallace was outgoing, and had the ability to make new friends readily. For example, after being introduced to Gisborne, a newcomer from Ottawa, Wallace invited him home for social occasions, including Christmas dinner, and the two started to meet sometimes for lunch. Although Wallace had always had many friends, he seemed this year especially to seek out new acquaintances. Perhaps he was tired of the "same old bunch," his description of the crowd with whom he had been socializing for years?

~

Walked down street with Mr. Gisborne of Ottawa — asked him to come out to our house tomorrow evening for a game of cards. Connie Fernau introduced him to me. Wednesday Nov. 27/12

Still foggy. 1:20. Had lunch with Gisborne at the Queen Lunch Rooms and dropped into the cine

afterwards & saw some of the Balkan War pictures.
8:30 Mac, Hume Hilton & Gerald Heath came out to
the house; had a musical evening. Monday Dec. 9/12

1 P.M. My cousin Wilbur dropped in to see me. He is
out here on his honeymoon. 1:10 Gisborne called in
to take me to lunch. I asked him to have tea with us
on Sunday. Friday Dec. 13th/12

3:30 Gisborne came out to tea, also Miss Hornby.
4 P.M. Arthur & I called at my uncle's, stayed for the
evening. Sunday Dec. 15th/12

9 P.M. Miss Cuthbertson's dance. Had a good time.
Nora Farrell, Margot Whitney, Dulcie (the same old
bunch). Walked home afterwards, got to bed 2:45.
Tuesday Dec. 17th/12

~

In the Christmas season, Wallace especially missed
Cecie, but gathered his friends around him for special
meals and gift-giving.[5]

~

Very jolly Xmas, but I wish Cecie's letter had come
today. I would have been happier. Presents were
simply showered on my sisters and me. Fred,
Gisborne, Robertson & A.L.B. in for dinner —
7 o'clock. The turkey was excellent and so was the
champagne. Wed. Dec. 25/12

Mac & Fred, Harold & Ian in for 10 o'clock supper of a fine goose served cold. Sat. Dec. 28/12

~

While Wallace spent much of his time in the company of male friends, and did not mention seeing Eugenie often, he recorded seeing Mrs. Schwengers from Victoria (Mrs. S. or C.S.) frequently. Sometimes she was in Vancouver, and apparently unescorted. When she attended the South African Campaigner's Ball in March, Wallace was exuberant about the evening, and gallantly escorted her home in a horse-drawn carriage. Other times, Wallace saw her in Victoria — for example, on the occasion when he attended the Government House Ball and visited Cecie's sister, Mrs. Hall, and her brother, Connie.

~

South African Campaigner's Ball, Lester Hall —
Military. Had a glorious time. Took Mrs. S. home in a
brougham — lovely bright night. The drive home was
delightful. Friday March 1st/12

C.S. left on noon boat for Victoria. Mon. Mar. 4th/12

Had lunch with Connie and Mrs. Hall at her house.
3 P.M. Went motoring with Mrs. Schwengers out by
Cordoba Bay. The country around Victoria is
beautiful. 9 P.M. took Connie, Mr. & Mrs. Hall to
Theatre. 12 P.M. Left for home. Fri. Apr. 19th/12

~

In October, Mrs. Schwengers (soon to become the more familiar "Chris") returned for another dance, again without an escort, and phoned Wallace to remind him to be there. Did Wallace walk her home after the dance? He did not say. But if he did, perhaps she was a surrogate for Cecie? Whatever Wallace's relationship with Chris, they were soon writing letters to each other and telephoning, in addition to seeing each other often.

⌒

Still cold. East wind. Mrs. Schwengers of Victoria is in town. She rang me up today, to see if I were going to the Ball tonight. Went to the dance, had a jolly time. Walked home afterwards — fine clear night — thought of Cecie & wished she were here.
Tuesday Oct. 22/12

9:30 Went down to the "Princess Sophia" to see Chris Schwengers off to Victoria. Wed. Oct. 23/12

Letter from C.S. In the evening finished reading Sir Gibbie. The last half dozen chapters are very good. Answered C.S. letter. Tuesday Oct. 29/12

4:30 Tea with C.S. at Hotel Vancouver. Tuesday Nov. 5/12

Chilly. Snow halfway down Grouse Mt. Walked down the street tonight with C.S. Friday Nov. 8/12

Heavy rain, with cold east wind. C.S. rang up. Monday Nov. 11/12

*8 P.M. Skating Party. Sue & Fred, Connie Fernau,
Gisborne, Miss Barnard, Mrs. Schwengers and
myself. Tuesday Nov. 12/12*

∿

One night, Chris phoned Wallace at the office, and he
walked her home the three and one-half miles. Although
it was not out of his way to walk her home — she was
staying with friends just a few blocks away from his
house[6] — why did they choose to walk? It was cool; they
could have taken a street car. It was apparent they
enjoyed each other's company. Or perhaps Chris was
troubled and wanted the occasion to talk? So far, in
Wallace's diary, there had been no mention of her
husband. The following night, Wallace took Chris to the
theatre. And the next night he recorded having "a very
good time" at his regimental dance, although he did not
mention the probable presence of Chris. Four nights later,
at the Rowing Club Ball, he rather stiffly noted the
presence of "Mrs. Schwengers," but also noted that he
took her home in a hansom cab at 3:30 A.M.

Chris Schwengers seemed to be available for companion-
ship with Wallace. What were his feelings? There did seem
to be a surreptitious nature to their relationship. For
instance, he received Chris's letters at the office, and read
them at 9:00 A.M. Cecie's letters were received and
acknowledged at 6:00 P.M., after he arrived home. And in
December, Wallace wrote Chris a letter "I shouldn't have
written."

∿

6 P.M. C.S. rang up. We walked home together, 3 1/2 miles. Spent the evening reading. 10:30 Went to bed. White frost tonight. Wednesday Nov. 13/12

8 P.M. Took C.S. to Theatre to see Quo Vadis. It is a fine play and well acted. Thursday Nov. 14/12

72nd Highlanders Dance in the armouries. Had very good time. Friday Nov. 15/12

11 A.M. Walked down to Westminster Tram with C.S. Saturday Nov. 16/12

Rain again. Met C.S. on street. Monday Nov. 18/12

Rowing Club Ball, Lester Hall. Met Eileen Green again, also Ailie Stuart & her aunt Mrs. Cowan, Girlie Townley was there & Mrs. Schwengers from Victoria. Had jolly good time, got home 3:30 in a Hansom Cab with C. Tues. Nov. 19/12

Walked down to the boat with Mrs. Schwengers. Walked back with Harold Marshall. Wed. Nov. 20/12

9:00 Letter from C.S. 2 nice letters from Cecie today. Jove! I'm feeling good. Tues. Dec. 3/12

Frosty. Ordered 2 dz. roses from Floral Hall, Brighton to be sent to Cecie for X'mas. 9/- Wrote to C.S. a letter I shouldn't have written. I have been thinking of Cecie all day. Wed. Dec. 4/12

~

Military Activities

This year, Wallace's military activities in the winter and spring consisted mostly of shooting practices and competitions. He was also on the regimental grass hockey team, which continued to be defeated. In February, labour conditions deteriorated in Vancouver; and the regiment stood "at the ready," but fortunately was not required.

~

3:30 Hockey match 72nd vs Vanc at Brockton Point. They defeated us 9-0. Sat. Jan. 20th/12

The 72nd warned to be ready to turn out if necessary to quell the Rioters. Sun. Feb. 4th/12

D Co'y Shoot. My score 60. Beat Mungall by 2. Feb. 27th/12

"D" Co'y shoot at miniature ranges. My score 58; Mungall 59; Abel 42; Borland 38; Bell Irving 69; Wrightson 63; Spence 60; Oliphant 48. Possible of 70. Tue. Mar. 5th/12

D Co. Shoot vs E Co'y. E won by 38 points. My score only 58 out of 70. Tue. Mar. 19th/12

10:30 Informal opening of Sergeant's Mess. 72nd Highlander's Quarters in Hoffmeister Bldg, 1155 Pender St. West. Tue. Mar. 26th/12

8 P.M. D Company parade. Lecture by Capt. Moore on advanced & rear guards. Sgt's Mess till 11:30. Tue Apr. 30th/12

~

Like most soldiers, Wallace did a lot of marching and was subject to many inspections. On one occasion, he noted that his battalion had been joined by the Duke of Connaught's Own Rifles (D.C.O.R.) for an all-day march. He was so enthusiastic that he acquired two recruits for the regiment.

~

Clear, warm. 10 A.M. Battalion parade. Marched to Kerrisdale. Held Divine Service. Afterwards skirmishing, advanced, rear guards. Returned 5 P.M. Sun. May 19th/12

Got 2 recruits for the 72nd Seaforths — Carter & Aitken, both nice chaps. Monday June 3rd/12

Quite hot. 72nd Reg't parade at 9:45 A.M. March to Kerrisdale. The 6 D.C.O.R went with us. Returned 5:30 P.M. Sun. June 16th/12

Right half Battalion parade at 8:30 P.M. A, B, C, & D Co'ys. Mon. June 17th/12

Battalion parade 8:15 P.M. We are to entertain the Sgts of the D.C.O.R in our Mess after parade. Got home 1:30 A.M. Thursday June 20th/12

Garrison Inspection parade 72nd Highlanders, 6th D.C.O.R. 18th F.A. by Major General Mackenzie. Sun. June 23rd/12

~

In late June, the reserve soldiers sailed to Vancouver Island for an arduous "route march" and a mock battle. Then the battalion travelled for a good will tour to Tacoma, Washington, for the U.S. July 4 celebrations.

～

Spent the evening at the armouries fitting out the chaps in D Co'y with Equipment for the route march. We are leaving on Friday noon per S.S. Princess Royal for Vancouver Island. Wed. June 26th/12

Left for Cowichan Bay 2 P.M. Arrived 7 P.M. & marched 4 miles to camp. Turned in 11 P.M. but none of us slept much. Up again at 4:30. Fri. June 28th/12

Marched about 16 miles today, through very pretty country about half the way it was uphill. Malahat Hill — camped at summit. Sat. June 29th/12

Marched to Goldstream. Delightful place. 2 P.M. Divine Service conducted by Captain the Rev. C.C. Owen, chaplain of the 6th D.C.O.R. Sunday June 30th/12

Met the enemy near Colwood — but D.Co'y was rear guard so we didn't do any firing. Marched on to the Barracks at Rod Hill & to Macaulay Plains. Left there for Victoria at 9 P.M. Left Victoria at midnight. Monday July 1st/12

Got home 6 A.M. pretty tired & feet blistered & very sore. Tue. July 2nd/12

The 72nd battalion leave for Tacoma, U.S.A. today at 7 P.M. We have been invited to spend the 4th of July there. We expect to have a jolly good time. The S.S. Princess Royal was chartered to take us down.
Wed. July 3rd/12

The Tacoma people gave us a great reception. They thought we were the best drilled regiment they had ever seen. Left there at 10:30 P.M. Thurs. July 4th/12

~

Wallace was a sergeant, but ambitious to climb the ladder. He wanted to be a commissioned officer, but that cost money, and Wallace had other things on which he spent his money. The Balkan situation was unstable, and even at this early stage, war between England and Germany was being talked about. The Minister of the Militia who spoke to Wallace's regiment in August may have been rallying the troops for just such an event.

~

I am looking forward to getting a commission in the Highlanders. It was offered me two years ago but I couldn't spare the necessary money. The uniform costs about $400.00. Sat. July 6th/12

Inspection of 72nd today at 2:30. Field Service dress. I took charge of the right half Company & moved them about for the D.O.C. Sat. July 13th/12

There is a general feeling these days that war between England and Germany is inevitable.
Tue. July 23rd/12

8 P.M. Went to reception to Col. Hughes, Minister of the Militia, in Pender Hall. He made a very good speech. Tuesday Aug. 6/12

8:30 "D" Co'y meeting. Got another recruit for the company, Alexander Aitken — stands 6 feet tall. All the men in "D" Co'y are 6 feet. Tuesday Aug. 27/12

3 P.M. Meeting of officers & sergeants at armouries to arrange guard of honour, etc. for Duke of Connaught. Sunday Sept. 8/12

3 P.M. The Duke reviewed the Garrison. Presented 72nd Colours. They were consecrated by Rev. John McKay, Chaplain. The Duke addressed us & led us in 3 cheers for King George. Thursday Sept. 19/12.

The Balkan War is on — looks serious. Friday Oct. 18/12

Quite frosty. Came in with Capt. Godson. We talked about the probability of Gt. Britain being involved in war rising out of the Balkan affair. Thursday Nov. 14/12

∽

H.R.H. Duke of Connaught's Visit to Vancouver, September 19, 1912
(Photo credit: Vancouver Public Library collection, #2025)

~

Notes

1. Throughout this book, for the sake of brevity, I have selected samples from Wallace's voluminous diary entries. Certainly it would have been impossible to include all of Wallace's references to the letters and post cards sent and received at this stage of his and Cecie's romance.

2. At this time, Fred Townley was an architect. He was living at home after completing his studies in the U.S.A.

3. My mother Gertie's engagement to Wilfred Middleton became another unmentionable topic in the family.

4. There was no mention in the diary that Wallace ever prepared meals himself.

5. In his monthly accounting, Wallace lists spending for Christmas presents: $2.50 + $8.00 + $4.50, and for E.B. (Eugenie Brünn), a lace handkerchief for 90 cents.

6. In his list of addresses, Chris was Mrs. Schwengers: 2337 1st Ave. West; phone Bayview 1081R. Wallace lived a few blocks west and south, thus to walk Chris home was not out of his way.

Chapter 7

~

1913

"A Lovely Letter From Cecie"

In 1913, Vancouver, and indeed Canada, was experiencing a recession, apparently due to pre-war jitters. The Balkan situation remained very unstable.[1] Evans, Coleman & Evans, Wallace's firm, felt the effects of this recession, and was laying off employees. Fortunately for Wallace, he was kept on. Engaged to Cecie, whom he had not seen for eight years, Wallace despaired about the financial plight which prevented him from travelling to England to marry her. Loneliness and frustration were dominant features of his life as he watched more and more of his friends get married. He credited his Christian faith, bolstered by his attendance at church, for assuaging his anxieties and guiding his decision-making. On happier ground, he continued to enjoy family, outdoor, social, and cultural activities. This was the last year Wallace kept a diary.

Work
In January, Wallace was given a new job description which involved his being outside most of the time. As

someone who loved being outdoors, this change suited him greatly.

~

Mr. Russell rang up. He wants me to confine my time to the cement and plaster end of the business. This will keep me outside most of the time, meeting the contractors, which I like doing. Jan. 28/13

Left my office at 407 Granville to take up new work calling on architects, contractors, etc. Jan. 30/13

Went to Kerrisdale this afternoon to arrange lecture on Good Roads. Mr. Johnson the Municipal Engineer is a nice chap. Thursday March 27/13

Scarcity of money these days — all Western Canada is affected. Business is quiet in Vancouver. The Balkan War is said to be the cause. March 28th/13

~

Although large orders for cement, plaster and other building materials were hard to come by, luckily there were some — for instance, the municipalities decided to spend some money on roads, including the paving of the Kingsway, and T.O. Townley began building a new house at Deer Lake in the fall.[2] Wallace was grateful to have his job when others were losing theirs, but was disappointed that he could not count on a raise at Christmas.

~

Went to Burnaby with Mr. Rochester to interview the council in the interest of concrete base for roads to be paved. They are going to spend $500,000.00 on roads this year. April 26/13

Went to New Westminster to see about S.S. Marmion cargo for Can. Mineral Rubber Co. who are paving Kingsway. May 26th/13

Got a big order from Champion & White. Complimented by Mr. Russell on my success, which is satisfactory to me. June 17/13

Business is very quiet. July 4/13

Had a chat with Mr. Russell. He told me that he was letting Finlay & Britton go at the end of this month on account of hard times. Thank the Lord he didn't discharge me, as it's very hard to get a good berth just now. Aug. 13/13

T.O. Townley is building a home at Burnaby Lake. E.C. & E. shipped the bricks, cement, plaster etc. Sept. 19/13

This has been a satisfactory day, as I feel I have accomplished a good deal for the firm. Oct. 13th/13

Not much doing in a business way these days. I fear the firm will not give any increases in salary this Christmas. Worse luck, as I for one, need it badly enough. Nov. 7/13

~

Real Estate Investments

Having purchased his home in Kitsilano the previous June, Wallace completed the paper work in the spring. He briefly considered making another real estate purchase in North Vancouver, no doubt wanting to augment his financial status with marriage in mind. Luckily for him, he couldn't finance the deal. Many Vancouverites who took the plunge regretted it, as property values soon experienced a prolonged drop.

~

Applied to have the property at 2532 Balaclava Rd. put in my name in the city assessment office. Also paid my water rates today — for half year ending June 30/13 — $4.20. Wed. Feb. 19/13

Nearly bought a lot in Hollyburn for $650.00, but find I can't finance it. I think it is a good investment for one who has the money. Wednesday Feb. 26/13

This is a glorious sunny spring day. One gets a beautiful view from Shaughnessy Heights on a clear day — there are some fine residences there — but it is fearfully hot up there in the summer — no trees. It will be much nicer in ten years. Thurs. Mar. 6/13

~

Wallace was not the only one looking at real estate. His sister, Edith, and her husband, Arthur, were thinking of buying a new home in North Vancouver. Apparently they found one, because in November, Wallace mentioned visiting them there. Wallace, however, was more preoccupied with his own problems. He was caught in a financial bind. He had made a commitment to Cecie, and had not seen her for eight years. He desperately wanted to embrace her, marry her, and bring her back to Vancouver.

At one point in April, Wallace was so anxious to go to England that he impetuously offered his Balaclava Road house to someone for a meagre $400 profit. He continued to hold the Grandview lot at Garden and East 10th Avenue, which was likely paid for. In any case, with fallen real estate values, he would not have been able to sell it. As further evidence of his frustration, in the fall, he was uncharacteristically expressing rancour about the people who had sold him the Balaclava house.

~

Another letter from Cecie. God bless her. Have been worrying about my finances. I really cannot see how I am going to be married and go on paying for the house — but I'll do it some way or other by God. Thurs. March 20/13

2:30 Arthur & I went to North Vancouver to look at a house he is thinking of buying. It is quite a nice place with a pretty garden. Friday March 21/13

Offered the house to a man today for $5000.00. My thoughts are always with Cecie. By Jove! I wish I could manage to go to England this summer. Wed. April 2/13

The money stringency is being keenly felt in Vancouver, in fact in all of Canada. Monday Apr. 7/13

Letter from Cecie. Pay income tax. Payment on house due today. Pd. Melekov 321.00, 33.65 interest a/c house 2532 Balaclava. Tues. June 10/13

Pay taxes on Grandview lot. Also on 2532 Balaclava. Friday Sept. 5/13

Mortgage interest due today. Friday Oct. 17/13

Posted letter to Vernon Bros. last night advising them that I am unsatisfied with the house I bought from them, as I find it not on a lane corner, as they represented it to be at the time I agreed to take it. I think I will sue them for damages for misrepresentation. Thursday Oct. 23/13

1:30 Lunch at the Blanchet's, No. Vanc. Went for a delightful walk through the woods with Arthur. The air was fine, and very invigorating. Living up here has its advantages. Sun. Nov. 2/13

~

Military Activities

The Balkan turmoil continued. Greece and Turkey remained at odds, and Turkey experienced a *coup d'état*, overthrowing the Ottoman Grand Vizier. As a sergeant in the 72nd Seaforth Highlanders, Wallace continued to attend regular D Company parades, occasional battalion parade, and, more and more frequently, battle exercises. It did not escape Wallace's notice that while he and his regiment were carrying out mock battles in order to give them "an idea of actual warfare," soldiers in other parts of the world were fighting each other for real.

~

4 P.M. Got a letter today addressed to Captain Chambers. Ha! Ha! I hope to be some day. Jan. 22/13

D Co'y Parade. Lecture in the mess by Major Pottinger on the Balkan Situation. Feb. 7/13

Battalion left Armouries 10 P.M. A, B, & C Companies went ahead and took up a position by the Golf Club in Point Grey. The remainder attacked the position and succeeded in capturing. It was interesting and gives one an idea of actual warfare. After the engagement we were served coffee, and marched home, arriving about 6 A.M., pretty tired. Sat. June 7/13

2 P.M. Left for Victoria en route to camp at Sidney. Wed. June 25/13

Slept last night at the Balmoral Hotel. 3:30 Left by train for Sidney, arrived 4:30. Got into my uniform & to camp by 6. Thurs. June 26/13

In camp were the 88th Fusiliers, 6th D.C.O.R, 72nd Seaforths, 104 Infantry. 10 A.M. We were inspected by Sir Ian Hamilton & Col. the Hon. Sam Hughes, Minister of the Militia. Friday June 27/13

Up at 5:30. Battalion drill in the morning. Afternoon sports. I pulled in Tug of War team. We won from the 104th — and got a prize in the 100 yard race. Sat. June 28/13

9 A.M. Church Parade. Drum head service. 5 P.M. Ran into Victoria with Black, had dinner & came out again at 7:30. Met Capt. Eades Ward in Victoria & came back with him. Sun. June 29/13

Heavy rain. 12 noon: Left camp & marched 12 miles to Elk Lake through beautiful country. Bivouacked in a lovely spot & enjoyed sleeping in the open, very much. The stars shone brilliantly. I was thinking of Cecie. Mon. June 30/13

Left Bivouac at 7 A.M. Came in touch with the enemy at Cordova Bay. Good practice at skirmishing all day. Got home feeling tired and dirty at midnight. Tues. July 1/13

War is still going on in the Balkans. The Greeks and Serbs are fighting each other now. July 3/13

~

After some indecisiveness, Wallace displayed a rare bit of acrimony in turning down a commission proffered to him in the Irish Fusiliers.

~

Cap't Dowding asked me if I would take a commission in the Irish Fusiliers. I'm afraid I can't afford it. I need all the money I can scrape together for my marriage next year to Cecie. God bless her. July 14/13

Have decided not to take commission in the Irish Fusiliers, partly because I haven't a high regard for the Colonel & Senior Major, & partly because I can use the money to better advantage, as I'm being married next year D.V. Aug. 14/13

Speaking to Cap't Dowding this A.M. He is very anxious about me taking a commission in the Irish

*Fusiliers. The Colonel will arrange terms for me to
pay for the uniform. I don't think I'll do it though, as
I don't like Col. McSpadden, nor Major Crehan
either. Aug. 30/13*

∽

The harsh economic climate was creating labour unrest,
and in August, Wallace's regiment was mobolized to
intervene if striking miners in Nanaimo rioted.

∽

*The regiment was ordered to mobilize, to proceed to
Cumberland to Quell the Riot. The miners are on
strike, causing trouble. We left last night at 12 o'clock.
Friday Aug. 15/13*

*Slept last night in the school house on the floor, with
our clothes on — didn't sleep very well.
Saturday Aug. 16/13*

*Left Cumberland for Union Bay & thence by steamer
to Nanaimo where we have been ordered. Pitched
camp in Nanaimo on the high ground opposite the
Post Office, overlooking the harbour.
Sunday Aug. 17/13*

*9 P.M. Great excitement. We expected the mob to start
trouble, so we lined up and the men all fixed
bayonets & got their ammunition ready. We scared
them evidently, as they were not long in dispersing.
Monday Aug. 18/13*

*The water at Nanaimo is beautifully clean and buoyant. Simply delicious for swimming.
Thursday Aug. 21/13*

Reveille at 5:30. Swimming at 6. By Jove it was great. Prison Escort at 9:30. I was Battalion orderly sergeant today. Friday August 22/13

Left Nanaimo 4 P.M. Col. Hall inspected us before leaving. Fine sail across the Gulf. Arrived home about 7 P.M. Very tired, had a bath & went to bed at 9 o'c. Friday Aug. 29/13

~

At the fall meeting of the Sergeant's Mess, Wallace was re-elected to the Board of Management.

~

8:30 Sergeants Mess Meeting. Election of Officers. I was re-elected for the Board of Management. Pres. Cl. Ser't Guttridge; Treas. Staff Serg't Masson; Sec'y Staff Serg't Newberry. Oct. 14/13

~

Family

Wallace's sister, Sue, and Fred Townley (F.L.T.) had set September 10 as the date for their wedding, with sister Gertie as bridesmaid. Wallace faithfully recorded the comings and goings of the Chambers and Townley families as they prepared for Sue and Fred's wedding. Fred continued to be a frequent visitor to the Chambers' household; several times a week, Wallace recorded that F.L.T. had been in to dinner or to play cards.

~

Sue & Fred have begun to buy their furniture — they are to be married in September. Jan. 7/13

8:30 F.L.T. came in. We played cribbage for an hour. Jan. 8/13

4 P.M. Mac & Gordon, Meyers & Robertson, Fred came in for tea. Gordon & Fred stayed for supper. Feb. 2/13

8:30 Sue & I won a rubber of Bridge from Gertie & Fred. Feb. 20/13

4:30 Mrs. Norrie, Fred, Percy MacLean & Arthur in to tea. April 6/13

Mrs. Townley called at the house today. May 17/13

9 P.M. Townley's for supper. Dr. & Mrs. McIntosh, Rev. Mr. Edwards of St. James & Bonnie & his bride were there. Sunday June 1/13

Noel Hunt came in last night. We had a jolly game of Bridge, Arthur & I winning from Fred Townley & Noel. Saturday June 14/13

Sue & Gertie went to the Townley's for Tea this afternoon. Sunday July 13/13

~

Like any brother, Wallace worried that the weather would mar his sister's wedding day. All went well, however, except that Wallace had a little too much champagne.[3]

~

4:30 Mrs. Townley, Girlie & Vi called.
Monday Sept. 1/13, Labour Day Holiday

We went out to see Sue's house in Kerrisdale. Very nice little place. 9 P.M. Supper party at the Townley's. Sue, Gertie, & I. Dorothy Follows, Violet, Mr. Follows (City Engineer), Fred, Bonnie, & Girlie. Very nice supper, although I should have stayed at home & written to Cecie. Sunday Sept. 7/13

Raining again — worse luck. Cleared up — fine afternoon. Sue has had heaps of beautiful presents sent her — sterling silver and cut glass galore. Sept. 8/13

Sue's wedding day. 12 Noon. Sue & Fred were married in St. James by Rev. Mr. Edward. Sue looked very pretty, and so did Gertie and Girlie as Bridesmaids. A large number of people were there, and about 50 of us went up to the Townley's for a breakfast, Toasts, etc. Afterwards C.R. Townley, Bonnie & Holmes Walker & I went to the Strand, where we had four bottles of champagne. Wednesday Sept. 10/13

Everyone said it was a very pretty wedding. The church was decorated with flowers. Sue & Fred surprised us by coming in to dinner. They boarded the boat for Alaska at Victoria & didn't know it called

*here for a few hours. It is a fine trip to Alaska. I'm
sure they will enjoy it. Thurs. Sept. 11/13*

*I can still feel the effects of the champagne — my
nerves are a bit "jumpy". I'll not be so silly next time
— one or two glasses will do me hereafter. We are
going to E.R. Townley's, Sylvia Court tonight for
dinner. Sept 12/13*

~

After a trip to Prince Rupert, a port on the way to
Alaska, the honeymooners returned. Once Sue and Fred
had occupied their new house, the rounds of visiting
apparently resumed, but received few more mentions
from Wallace.

~

*8:30 Sue & Fred are back from their honeymoon.
They enjoyed the trip to Prince Rupert immensely.
Sept. 16/13*

Sue moved into her new house at Kerrisdale. Sept. 22/13

*Dinner party at our place: Mr. & Mrs. F.L. Townley,
Miss Agnes Martin, & Mr. Guy Blanchet. Mr. & Miss
Bois came in afterwards. Sept. 29/13*

~

Social Activities

The year started with a surprise for Wallace. His good
friend Dulcie was engaged! She had been one of the first
that he told about his own engagement. Soon several of

his long-time friends were engaged or married. This only intensified his anguish about being apart from Cecie.

~

Sue & I & F.L.T. went to the Smith's. They are now in their fine big house in Shaughnessy Heights. During the evening, Dulcie's engagement was announced, to Mr. Bodwell — which surprised me greatly. He is a nice chap — a civil engineer. Friday Jan. 3/13

Seaforth Highlanders Regimental Ball. Sally Davis rang up. She is now Mrs. Billy Marshall. I haven't seen her for two years. She is going to the Ball tonight. The dance went off very well. I got to bed 3 A.M. Snowing. Friday Jan. 10/13

10:00 Dulcie phoned up to ask me there tonight for a game of Bridge. Lilo Cuthbertson will be there, also Mr. Pegram, her fiancé. The Hornby's are at 1112 Cardero now. Saturday Feb. 1/13

Imperial Club dance. Lilo Cuthbertson sent us invitation. Had jolly time. Miss Reeve looked charming. She is a new girl. Sue looked sweet too. Lent begins tomorrow, so no gayety for a while. I'm not sorry either. Tuesday (Shrove) Feb. 4/13

~

In February, Wallace heard from Clare Battle, who was living in Victoria. Since the tapering off of their relationship in 1911, his diary had not mentioned her. Wallace recorded that he and Clare met at least a few times before she, too, was married.

～

1:30 Lunch with F.L.T. Had a note from Clare Battle from Victoria. She will be over tomorrow. She & Mrs. Burge invited me to tea with them at the Vancouver Hotel, Sunday afternoon. Friday Feb. 7/13

Met Clare Battle on the street. She was on her way to the station — going to Edmonton on a holiday. Friday June 6/13

Lord Amassy! Clare B. is engaged. Rev. Canon Silva-White is the lucky man. Friday July 11/13

Got a nice note from Mrs. Silva-White (Clare Battle), thanking me for the wedding present. Thursday Oct. 9/13

2:15 Met Mrs. Silva-White (née Clare Battle) in Spencer's. She is looking well. Tuesday Dec. 16/13

～

Playing cards, eating out in the company of friends, musical evenings — and weddings — continued to be Wallace's most frequently mentioned social activities.

～

Gertie & I going to a little "Bridge" at the Lucas-Hunt's tonight. Peggy's fiancé will be there. Wednesday May 14/13

Had a jolly time at the Hunt's "Bridge". Miss Agassiz
was my partner but Mr. Hunt and Miss McPherson
beat us. Others there were: Mr. & Mrs. Lambert Bond,
Mr. & Mrs. Flower (great friends of Agnes Martin),
Mr. & Mrs. Cresswell, Mr. Ray (Peggy's fiancé), Harry
Michen & Teale. Fri. May 16/13

Lovely day. 1 P.M. to St. James to see Dulcie married
to Howard Lionel Bodwell C.E. Her brother Leyland,
and Geoff Hornby was groomsman. Margot Graveley
was married today at St. Paul's to Edward Munro
Craven McLorg. Babs MacPherson was Bridesmaid.
10:30 Glorious evening. I lay on the hammock
thinking of Cecie. Wed. July 30/13

1 P.M. Robbie & I lunched at the Strand. He is
accountant in the Canadian Bank of Commerce &
was moved up country some time ago, & is down
here on a holiday. I paid for the lunch & he bought
the wine which cost him $3.50. Wed. Sept. 3/13

7 P.M. Percy, Guy, & Gerald in to dinner. The Misses
Bois came in for the evening — Miss Hilda played the
violin, a piece called Fragment is very pretty. We
played games too. A very jolly evening. Friday Sept. 5/13

8:30 Bridge at Mrs. Brownings, Denham Court. It
was given in honour of Peggy Hunt who is to be
married shortly. I gave her a watercolour. Sat. Oct. 5/13

~

ENGAGEMENTS
The engagement is announced of Miss
Ethel Margaret Hunt, daughter of Mr.
and Mrs. Lucas Hunt of Vancouver, to
Mr. Lionel Victor Ray of the Canadian
bank of Commerce, and second son of
the late Charles Henry Ray, St. Cross
Mill, Winchester, and Mrs. Ray, now of
Fernleigh, Woolston, Southampton, England.

This newspaper clipping about Peggy Hunt's engagement
was saved in Wallace's diary.

In 1913, Wallace and his sisters saw the Bois family
often. Hilda Bois was probably a friend of Gertie's.

~

*Miss Bois, Hilda, and Mr. B. in for dinner. Maude &
Mr. B. played Bridge with Miss Bois & I till 11:30.
Good game. Hilda played the violin very nicely.
Thurs. Nov. 6/13*

*8:30 Miss Bois asked me in for a game of Bridge. Met
Mr. Mickle. Wed. Dec. 3/13*

*8:30 Took Gertie & Hilda to dance at the Armouries.
Pretty good fun. I danced the Highland Schottische
for the first time with Dorothy Broadbent.
Sat. Dec. 13/13*

~

Eugenie Brünn had not been mentioned in Wallace's
1912 diary for several months. Early in January 1913,
however, Wallace visited Eugenie. As always, his diary
was not forthcoming. Perhaps it was an impulse? Did he

have tender feelings for her? Or she for him? Did he feel lonely for Cecie, and want some comfort from Eugenie? What his diary recorded was that they saw each other several times in the spring, and that seeing Eugenie sometimes resulted in fervent entries about his love for Cecie.

~

6:30 Called to see E.B. Sun. Jan. 5/13

8:30 Went to Orpheum with E.B. Fri. Jan. 17/13

8:30 Boy Scouts meeting at <u>Seymour School</u>. Met <u>E.B.</u> Sue & Gertie at Aunt Rose's party. I called for them at 11 o'c. Friday Jan. 31/13

8:30 Took E.B. to the Kinemacolor to see the naval pictures. Had a perfectly sweet letter from Cecie tonight with some snap shots. She is a <u>darling</u>. I adore her. Thursday Apr. 3/13

8:30 Called at E.B. Tuesday. <u>Beautiful</u> letter from Cecie. Tues. Apr. 8/13

~

After April, Wallace made no further notation about Eugenie until November, when he announced that she had been in Norway for the summer. They began seeing each other again, but Wallace soon had regrets. By mid-December, he was imploring God's help to "lead an upright noble life." The next day, after work, Wallace took

Eugenie to the Tea Kettle. Was it to declare his intentions not to see her again so that he could be true to Cecie?

~

Took Gertie to Miss Cowards dance. Miss Brünn was there. She has been in Norway all summer.
Tues. Nov. 4/13

8 P.M. Took E.B. to cine. Sat. Nov. 8/13

Raining heavily. 8:30 To Cine with E.B. (I wish I hadn't.) Sat. Nov. 15/13

11 A.M. Communion Service in St. John's. 1:30 Called to see E.B. Made a vow today & prayed to God that I might lead an upright noble life, for Christ's sake, and for Cecie's sake. <u>God help me</u>.
Sunday Dec. 14/13

4:45 Took Eugenie to tea at the "Tea Kettle".
Monday Dec. 15/13

~

On another front, Wallace had last heard from Chris Schwengers (C.S.) on December 3, 1912, and the next day sent "a letter I shouldn't have written." Chris sent a reply a few weeks later, but Wallace didn't mention her again until February 1913, when he enigmatically recorded that he saw "Mr. & Mrs. Bernie Schwengers" at a restaurant. This was the only time he ever mentioned Chris's husband.[4] Wallace and Chris continued to meet and to write each other regularly, especially in the summer while

Eugenie was away. Wallace's diary entries did not make clear the nature of his relationship with Chris, but at the same time they did not contain the kind of anguish which seemed to be part of his relationship with Eugenie this year. As with his entries about Eugenie, however, he sometimes juxtaposed his notation about Chris and his feelings about Cecie.

~

1:30 Sue & I lunched at Spencer's. Saw Mr. & Mrs. Bernie Schwengers there. Wed. Feb. 19/13

Went for a walk to the Park with C.S. Glorious night. I wish I could be with Cecie. Tuesday May 20/13

Fine & warm. 3:30 Went canoeing with C.S. Sat. May 24, 1913

My birthday (27 years). Got a lovely letter from Cecie, and two photos of her sweet self— in silver frames. Evelyn sent me a card too, also C.S. My sisters were sweet to me. Friday May 30/13

Fine & warm. Noon: got letter from Mrs. Schwengers asking me to go to Victoria tomorrow for a picnic she is getting up. I would like to go, but feel that I ought to go to communion on Sunday. Also I have to parade with the regiment at 10 P.M. for tonight's manoeuvres. Friday June 6, 1913

12 noon. Wrote to C.S. Friday June 20/13

2 P.M. Left for Victoria en route to camp at Sidney. 8 P.M. Went canoeing up the Gorge with C.S. It is

charming there. I will take Cecie some day.
Wed. June 25/13

~

Wallace gave no clue as to the contents of the letters he
and Chris sent each other. Perhaps they were simply to
arrange times when they could meet. Long-distance
telephone calls were not the norm in 1913; in fact,
Wallace still referred to them as "long distance wire."

~

Noon: Letter from C.S. Thursday July 10/13

I spoke to C.S. today over long distance wire.
Monday July 21/13

8 P.M. Called at the Vancouver Hotel for Mrs. Schwengers
& Mrs. Cane, also Mr. Kurt Betz, an awfully fine
chap, a German — very handsome. We all went to a
cine & then to Eng. Bay Pavilion where we had two
or three waltzes. It was great fun. Came back to the
Vancouver & listened to the orchestra till 11 P.M.
when the ladies retired, and Betz & I went to the
Windsor, had supper. Thurs. July 24/13

Betz is a very good tennis player. Mrs. Sch. &
Mrs. Cane both play well, & are playing in the
Tournament this week. Friday July 25/13

~

Before Chris Schwengers and Mrs. Cane returned to
Victoria the following Saturday on the midnight boat,

Wallace met Chris and they walked along Georgia Street. What did they discuss? Wallace gave no hint, but recorded that he went home and thought about Cecie. The following Monday, he wrote that he was thinking of "C.S." all day. Was it a Freudian slip? Or did he intend to write "C."(Cecie)?

~

9:00 Called at the Vancouver, met Mrs. Schwengers, went for a walk with her along Georgia Street & back, when we met Mrs. Cane. Betz & I accompanied them to the Victoria boat. We went down to the dock in a cab. Midnight: Cool. I sat on the verandah thinking of Cecie. I'm dying to see her. Sat. July 26/13

Thinking of C.S. all day. 6:30 Hurried home expecting a letter from Cecie. Was disappointed, but I'm sure it will come tomorrow. Mon. July 28/13

8:30 Called at the Dunsmuir to see Mrs. Schwengers & the Misses Frazer. Spent a pleasant evening. Home 11:30. Mon. Aug. 4/13

~

In September, Wallace noted that Chris had phoned him on the day of the Daughters of the Empire Ball, but he did not say that she attended. In any case, he went with his sister, Gertie, and was home early. Wallace, did, however, record seeing Chris three more times in 1913. The third entry, written on Hallowe'en, announced that Chris was moving to Vancouver and taking up a new career. Whether or not he continued to see her, this was the last time Wallace mentioned Chris Schwengers in his diary.

~

Daughters of the Empire dance. C.S. rang up. 9 P.M.
Jolly little dance. Met Miss Card & Miss Herman.
Gertie & I left at 11:30. Mrs. Hunt came home with
us. Fri. Sept. 26/13

8:30 went to Orpheum with C.S. Very good show this
week. Midnight: walked home from Talton Place.
Fine clear night. Wed. Oct. 1/13

8:30 Fine evening. Moon made it light, & the air
frosty. Mr. & Mrs. Duckworth, Mrs. Schwengers & I
went to the Orpheum. Enjoyed it awfully, & laughed
heartily. Mrs. D. could hardly stop & almost got
hysterical. Wed. Oct. 8/13

Hallowe'en. Fine & clear. Had a note from C.S. She is
going in to the Hospital here as a nurse.
Friday Oct. 31/13

~

Cultural Activities

This year, as in previous years, Wallace enjoyed
concerts, plays, and lectures — all complementing his
intellectual and social life.

~

8:30 Arthur & I went to Lecture illustrated with slides
of South America by Dr. G.W. Ray, F.R.G.S. It was
very interesting. The Incas were highly civilized —
centuries ago. Some of their temples etc. are wonder-
ful. Rio de Janeiro is a beautiful city.
Mon. Jan. 13/13

Mischa Elenan is playing tonight at the Imperial. Went to hear him. By Jove he plays beautifully — Concerto in F sharp, Zeigerweiser by Sarasate were my favourites. He played the well known Humoresq by Dvorak as an encore. Thurs. Feb. 27/13

3 P.M. St. John Mildmay's Lecture on Shakespeare. Tuesday March 18/13

Capt. Amundsen will tell of his experiences on his trip to the South Pole in the Arena tonight. Arthur & I went to hear Clara Butt & Kennerly Rumford last night. About 5000 people were there. She sings divinely and he has a splendid Baritone voice. I haven't enjoyed a concert as much for ages. She made me think how much we are missing by living way out here. Thurs. Apr. 10/13

Went to see a beautiful painting by De Morean, Cannes, France who died in 1893. "The Village Blacksmith". The effect of the firelight is magnificently executed. The picture is valued at $60,000.00. Wed. May 7/13

Geraldine Farrer at the Opera House. Mon. Sept. 29/13

∽

Books

Wallace and Cecie were both avid bibliophiles, and they continued to delight in reading and exchanging books. Some of Wallace's choices were: *A Man's Man* by Ian Hay; *The Trail of '98* by Robert Service; *The Expensive Miss DuCane* by S. MacNaughton; and Shakespeare's

Hamlet. One book he sent Cecie was Handford
Henderson's *John Percyfield,* which he read first, and from
her, he received such books as *The Greatest Wish in the
World* by E. Temple Thurston and *The Lady of the
Occasion,* which he pronounced *"a charming book . . .
very cleverly written."*

~

*Didn't get up till eleven. Reading "The City of
Beautiful Nonsense" by Thurston. Sunday Jan. 5/13*

*Had lovely long letter from Cecie yesterday, also 2
books "The Stumbling Block by J.M. Forman and
"Our Lady of the Beeches" by Baroness Van Hutton.
Friday Feb. 28/13*

*Started to read "Tom Brown's School Days".
Wed. June 11/13*

*Book from Cecie came today. "Where Love Is", by
Wm. J. Locke. Wed. July 16/13*

*Reading Ingoldsby Legends. To bed at 11:30
Mon. Nov. 24/13*

*Started to read one of Thackeray's books. Very good.
Wednesday Nov. 26/13*

*Finished reading "The Mirage" which is an excellent
story, a sweety sad sort of story. Monday Dec. 15/13*

~

Outdoors

This year, more of Wallace's outings were within the city limits, except for those associated with his military activities. During the summer, Wallace enjoyed swimming at the beach, but no more canoeing — in July, he had sold his canoe.

~

3:30 Arthur & I went for a walk in Stanley Park — which looked <u>beautiful.</u> The trees all covered with snow. God I wish Cecie could have seen it. As we walked home the moon came up & a very bright star. Enjoyed the walk very much. Sunday Jan. 12/13

Went for a walk with Maude in the afternoon — it was glorious walking — keen frosty air. Sunday Jan. 19/13

3:30 Went for a walk up Balaclava Rd. through the trees as far as 21st Avenue. Sunday May 18/13

Went canoeing for the first time this year. Heavens! If Cecie were here what glorious times we could have canoeing, etc. Thursday May 22/13

4 P.M. Rode around the Marine Drive on Arthur's bicycle. That is a perfect road through the most beautiful country. Sat. June 14/13

Glorious summer day. 11 A.M. Arthur & I went to St. Mark's & afterwards walked along Kitsilano Beach to MacDonald Street. Sun. June 22/13

*Sold the canoe to Percy MacLean for $30.00
Friday July 4/13*

*2:30 Very warm. Arthur & I, Sue, Gertie & Phyllis all
went to the beach at Bayswater St. & enjoyed the
bathing for an hour or so. A. & I had a race 100 yds.
I beat him by 10 ft. 7:30-9:00 Glorious sunsets.
Sat. July 19/13*

*Delightful swim at the beach at the foot of Bayswater St.
Sat. Aug. 9/13*

$\sim$

Now that Wallace was a home-owner, some of his time
outdoors was spent chopping wood and planting bulbs.

$\sim$

*Spent the day at home, digging up the garden &
planting bulbs. Monday Oct. 20/13 Thanksgiving
Day*

*I dug up the garden this afternoon, and split up a lot
of wood. I have caught a cold, I see. I must take some
Bromo-quinine. Motored up to Shaughnessy with
Larry Townley. Fine bright day. Sat. Nov. 1/13*

*2:30 to 5 P.M. Digging garden. Planted Hyacinths.
Sat. Nov. 8/13*

$\sim$

Church

Wallace continued to comment in his diary on the value of the messages he received from church sermons. In February, he recorded that a piece of music had been played in memory of Captain Robert Scott and two companions, who had died in Antarctica in their attempt to return from the South Pole.

~

7:30 Gertie & I went to St. John's, heard a very good sermon on Character. Sunday Jan. 26/13

7:30 St. John's Church. Very good sermon. They played Chopin's Funeral March in memory of Capt. Scott and his party. Miss McGuire sang beautifully. Sunday Feb. 16/13

The sermon last night impressed me very much and did me good. I feel in fine spirits today. Monday March 31/13

7:30 Went to church with Sue — very good sermon. I always feel <u>better</u> after church. Sunday April 6/13

Had dinner in town tonight with McGlashen. Had interesting talk on churches, religion, etc. I asked him to come to St. John's next Sunday. Tuesday Apr. 8/13

~

Wallace was struggling to come to terms with the reality that it was impossible for him to go to London and marry Cecie. At the same time, he may have been struggling to clarify his ongoing relationship with Chris Schwengers and his renewed relationship with Eugenie Brünn. Wallace counted on his religion to help him live an "honest, upright life."

∼

I have resolved to live an honest, upright life and have asked God to help me in my desire. It is easily seen that being honestly poor is much better than being dishonestly rich. Although I wish I had more money — for Cecie's sake. Wed. June 4/13

7:30 To St. John's. Very fine sermon by Dr. John Mackay on "Peace", deplored the tremendous sums spent by England & Germany & other nations on armaments. Sunday Dec. 21/13

∼

Cecie

Letters between the long-distance lovers continued to cross the Atlantic unabated. At the beginning of the year, much of Wallace's diary was taken up with choosing a ring for Cecie, both for her birthday and to commemorate their engagement the year before.

∼

Inspected rings at Allan's, Birks & Todd Mannings. I like Birks selection best. I can get a nice emerald and two diamonds for $100.00, which I have decided to take. Thurs. Jan. 9/13

Two nice letters from Cecie last night — one was written on New Year's Day & evidently she didn't get the roses I ordered to be sent to her on New Year's Eve. Friday Jan. 17/13

Picked out a ring today in Birks — they made it to my order — and is quite a nice emerald with a diamond on each side — $110.00. I will send it to Cecie to signify our betrothal. Tues. Jan. 21/13

I am not satisfied with the ring Birks made for me. The Emerald is too small in comparison to the diamonds. They are making another. Wed. Jan. 22/13

Chose ring today for Cecie, a pretty Emerald with a diamond on each side. Got it at Birks. Monday Feb. 3/13

Mailed ring today to Cecie, as I want it to arrive on or before the 23rd. Henry Birks & Sons mailed it; they insure it as well. The Emerald is a very nice one. I hope Cecie likes it. Thursday Feb. 6/13

4:30 Ordered 2 D. Roses from Floral Hall, Brighton to be sent to Cecie for her birthday. 6:30 Had a note from Cecie written from St. Winifred's, Bangor, Wales. Monday Feb. 10/13

6:30 Lovely letter from Cecie, also some P.P.C. from Wales. Thurs. Feb. 13/13

~

On Valentine's Day, Wallace seemed despondent. Sue and Fred were busily planning their fall wedding, and some of Wallace's friends were engaged or already married. His diary recorded his dismay about the vast distance separating him from his love, and his inability to bridge that gap. In February, Cecie enclosed letters from Harry Broadwood (H.B.), who last year had caused Wallace so much concern. But the issue was apparently resolved; Wallace noted the letters without comment.

⁓

I wish Cecie were out here. There is such a lot I want to talk to her about. Just imagine being engaged to a girl & not seeing her for over seven years. My word it's awful! And I'm so stupid at writing too. My letters are so short & dull. I almost wonder she doesn't complain. God bless her. Friday Feb. 14/13

6:30 2 letters from Cecie, enclosing some of H.B.'s. Wednesday Feb. 19/13

This has been a glorious day— bright sun. I was in North Vancouver this afternoon. The few minutes on the water going over were delightful. I tried to imagine I was crossing the Atlantic on my way to see Cecie. Thursday Feb. 20/13

This day a year ago I got Cecie's letter accepting me. This has been a lovely bright sunny day. I have been thinking of Cecie all day. 8:30 wrote to Cecie. Sunday Feb. 23/13

I wish I had enough money to go to England this year. I want to see Cecie very much. Wednesday Feb. 26/13

Ordered some flowers to be sent to Cecie for Easter. Monday Mar. 3/13

3 charming letters from Cecie — sent me a photo of herself & sisters & brothers taken 18 years ago. She looks sweet. Wednesday Mar. 5/13

3 letters from Cecie. She got the ring, but it was two days late. I intended it to reach her by the 23rd. She is a darling and I love her with all my heart and soul. Tuesday Mar. 11/13

Raining heavily. 6:30 Lovely letter from Cecie. Have felt in excellent spirits all day, and her letter made me unusually happy. Monday March 17/13

6 P.M. Letter from Cecie. God bless her. Monday April 14/13

~

Like any lovestruck person, Wallace was full of emotion. One day he seemed reconciled not to travel to see Cecie this year; the next, he was again yearning to go. A day without a letter from her could plunge him into the depths. And despite leading an active and outwardly happy life, Wallace wrote: *"I never enjoy anything completely though, as Cecie is not here."*

~

Gad! I wish I could afford to go to England. Hope to go next year though. Tuesday April 15/13

10-11 Sat in a reverie in front of the fireplace — thinking of the future with Cecie. Sunday Apr. 20/13

*10:30 Wrote a note to Cecie enclosing two pansies,
the first flowers picked from our garden.
Wed. Apr. 30/13*

*I keep thinking Cecie is sick. I do hope it is not true.
Only a short note from her this week. Friday May 2/13*

*Fine sunny morning. 6:30 Two charming letters
from Cecie. I am so happy to hear she has not been
ill. She is a darling. My word! I would like to go over
this year. Mon. May 5/13*

*8 P.M. <u>Writing to Cecie</u>. Didn't go to church. 10:30
Fine starry night — went for a short walk — thinking
of Cecie. Sun. May 18/13*

*Letter from Cecie. The photo did not come. It must
have gone astray. Tuesday May 13/13*

*8 A.M. Motored to Clayburn (55 miles) with F. W.
Foster & Mr. Spifford of the Nichols Chemical Co.
Went up 3 1/2 hours. Had lunch at the Purver's
ranch. They have a lovely place — every kind of
flower imaginable. They served a very nice lunch.
Started back at 3 P.M. Got here at 6. The country is
beautiful. I wd like to have taken Cecie on this trip.
Thurs. May 29/13*

*At 5 P.M. went to English Bay & watched the bathers
disporting themselves for an hour. It is glorious down
there. I never enjoy anything completely though, as
Cecie is not here. Sat. May 31/13*

*8:30 Arthur & I walked to the end of MacDonald
Street where there is a lovely grassy spot overlooking*

English Bay. The sunset was glorious. I thought how delightful it would be to take Cecie to see it. Maybe I will next year. Wed. June 18/13

I spent this day very happily with Cecie 8 years ago. Thinking of Cecie. Saturday July 12/13

10 P.M. Went to the foot of Balaclava St. & watched the huge waves roll in. I loved the wildness & roar. I thought of Cecie, as she would love it too. Wed. Aug. 6/13

Fine summer weather. God. Why can I not have Cecie here, to enjoy these delightful days with me? Friday Aug. 8/13

~

By the fall, Wallace finally faced the unpleasant fact that he could not afford to travel to England to be married. His solution? If they were to make their home in Vancouver, why not be married there? In October, he asked Cecie to do just that.

~

2 lovely letters from Cecie. She mentioned Mr. Starkey. It worries me that I am not able to be in London. I want to see her so very much. Of course, I do not object to seeing him as he knows we are engaged, and he is a gentleman. Monday Sept. 15/13

A lot of P.P.C.s from Cecie, of Canterbury Cathedral & Birmingham. Very interesting. Tuesday Sept. 16/13

Letter from Cecie. She enclosed samples of her new dress. I'm sure the colour will suit her & she will look charming in it. I hope she sends me a photo.
Wed. Sept. 24/13

7:30 It is cold and wet outside tonight and I have just finished dinner & am now sitting in front of the fireplace in a comfortable chair, smoking my old pipe. Jove, how much I have to be thankful for. Had a sweet note from Cecie too, which I have just read. What a magnificent girl she is. Monday Oct. 6/13

6:30 Dinner. Disappointed — no letter from Cecie. Spent the eve. reading. It was a glorious moonlight night. I wish I could have gone for a walk with Cecie, as it reminded me of that night in Blairmore, after the circus, 8 years ago. Heavens how the time flies. Mon. Oct. 13/13

9:30-11:30 Writing to Cecie. Mentioned that I might not be able to go to England, asked her if she would come out. Mon. Oct. 20/13 Thanksgiving Day

～

Although he did not say so in his diary, Wallace must have worried about the possible consternation of Cecie's family when they heard that her husband-to-be was so poor that he must ask his bride to be married thousands of miles from her home. A long month after Wallace asked her, Cecie finally wrote that she agreed with the idea of coming to Canada. Wallace's diary recorded no concrete plans for how to accomplish this goal. Perhaps they were going to ask her parents for help in lieu of a London wedding?

~

Felt blue today. Cecie's letter cheered me, though. God bless her. Raining heavily. Monday Nov. 17/13

Note from Cecie telling me her Uncle George died on Nov. 5. Wednesday Nov. 19/13

Thinking a lot of Cecie these days — these will be sad days for her — and her aunt & Violet. Friday Nov. 21/13

Cox won the Salmon Sweepstake ($28,000.00) — lucky beggar. I wish I had, in which case it wouldn't take me long to get to London. 9:30 Wrote to Cecie. Monday Nov. 24/13

Had a lovely letter from Cecie. She is quite willing to come out here to be married. I am so glad. Of course, I would like to have gone to London, but I really can't afford it. Wed. Nov. 26/13

~

Now that Wallace and Cecie had decided that she would travel to Vancouver to be married, Wallace focused on how to afford Christmas gifts.[5]

~

Ordered 2 dozen roses to be sent to Cecie for Christmas, from L. Prockter, Brighton. Monday Dec. 1/13

7 P.M. Nice letter from Cecie. It puzzles me to know what to send Cecie for Xmas, as I can't afford very much. Thurs. Dec. 4/13

Evening down town to buy Xmas Cards. I wish I could have bought something <u>very</u> nice for Cecie. Sat. Dec. 6/13

Wrote to Cecie — Xmas letter. 11:30 To bed in good spirits. The sermon did me good tonight. Sunday Dec. 7/13

2 letters from Cecie today. Bought a sterling silver jewel case for Cecie, CEF engraved on the top. Also ordered 1 1/2 doz Chrysanthemums to be del'd on New Year's. Tuesday Dec. 9/13

~

Wallace ended his 1913 diary on a high note. He had sent Christmas letters and gifts to Cecie, and had received letters and gifts from her in return, including a home-made cake over which he was rapturous in his praise. On New Year's Eve, he had every hope not only of seeing Cecie in 1914, but of finally marrying her, and starting his adult life.

~

Got lots of nice things. Card & letter from Cecie. In the afternoon I went to my room & lay on my bed for an hour, thinking of Cecie. Thurs. Dec. 25/13

Fine clear day. Beautiful sunrise this morning. It makes me feel good. Got a Gillette Safety Razor from Cecie — the dear girl — & a strop too. 6:30 Letter *from Cecie, and a cake — <u>beautifully</u> iced and oh! how delicious. 10:30 Wrote to Cecie, thanking her. Clear frosty night. This has been a <u>very</u> happy day for me. Mon. Dec. 29/13*

8:30 I spent the evening at the Bois. At midnight we sang Auld Lang Syne. I feel very elated over the birth of the New Year, as 1914 will mean so much to me. 12:30 Took a hot bath & to bed. My thoughts are with Cecie. Wed. Dec. 31/13

~

Notes

1. The Balkan War was about to resume. The Greeks would capture thousands of Turks at Janina.

2. By fall, Townley was sister Sue's father-in-law. More information about Deerholme, the Townley home, can be found in the *Deer Lake Park Heritage Resource Inventory* published by the City of Burnaby Community Heritage Commission in 1998 (page 19).

3. Wallace spent $10 on a wedding present for Fred and Sue, and $5 for the champagne.

4. On December 7, 1946, the *Victoria Colonist* noted the death of Bernhard P. Schwengers, who left a widow. His Last Will and Testament names her as Beatrice May Schwengers. Thus two possibilities exist: Chris Schwengers may have not been the Mrs. Schwengers noted on this occasion, or she was his wife prior to a later marriage. The latter seems likely.

5. Wallace's December cash account shows the cost of the roses to be $5, and the mums, $1.50.

Chapter 8

~

1914

"Won't It Be Fine Seeing Cecie Again"

On July 28, 1914, World War I intervened in the plans of Wallace and thousands of other young men and women. By September, Wallace was in Quebec and on his way overseas with the 16th Battalion. His good-bye note to Gertie showed some trepidation. Would he be allowed to write letters "from there"? In spite of whatever worries he might have had, he could not hide his exuberance about soon being reunited with Cecie after nine years.

~

16th Battalion, 4th Brigade, Valcartier, P.Q.
Sept. 23rd, 1914

Dear Gertie,

Just a few lines to say goodbye as we are off in the morning. We are going to march in to Quebec and embark from there for England. I hope to be able to write from there, but am not sure whether it will be allowed. Won't it be fine seeing Cecie again — Jove, I'm so excited already.

I do hope you will be well, Gertie, and happy. I'll be thinking of my sisters, and how good they have always been to me.

Love to you all, Wallace

~

After Wallace reached London, and finally saw Cecie, he sent a jubilant post card to his sister, Edith.

~

Salisbury Plains, Oct. 30, 1914

Had a glorious time in London. C. is <u>adorable</u>. Enjoying life here very much. The country about here is beautiful. Don't get much time for writing. Love to Phyllis and Arthur.

~

Wallace and Cecie were married on December 19, 1914. His best man was Lieut. James M. McKerral, who had enlisted in Vancouver for active duty on the same day as Wallace.

Wallace's departure to the war zone was delayed until he completed a course at Hythe, in the county of Kent, on the shore of the English Channel. The course trained him as a machine gunner — a far cry from the young man who loved music, books, and plays. Let us imagine that his bride was in close propinquity during those fleeting weeks. Unfortunately, there is no documentation of that short phase of their life.

Wallace and Cecie, 1914

Lieut. Wallace Chambers,
72nd Seaforth Highlanders, November 1914

Postscript

~

In 1990, my wife, Marion, and I were part of a tour group of World War I sites throughout Belgium and France. In Armentières, we found Wallace's grave in a British cemetery.

The grave of Wallace Chambers, 1990

I have very little information about Cecie. A few months after Wallace's death, she moved to London, England, where she remained, one of the thousands of childless war-widows. I know only that she died many years later.

The following letter is the only one I have from the time after Wallace died. Cecie wrote it to Wallace's sister, Maude, some time in the fall of 1915. The "Harold" Cecie mentioned was Wallace's cousin, Uncle George Gibson's son; "Nona" was Cecie's younger sister.

~

Orthopedic Hospital
234 Great Portland Street,
London W.
Men's Ward

Maude dearest,

Your letter and lovely book (One of Miller's) came a few days ago. I wish I could tell you how much I love it and how much it helps me.

If this letter is disjointed please forgive me as the men have the gramophone going full blast and the noise is awful. It was my day off on Friday so I went off duty at 6:30 Thursday night and went home to sleep. Alice came up for the night, so Evelyn, she and I were lazy as we could be, in fact I didn't get up until 1 o'clock and we all had lunch in our dressing gowns as we were alone. Well, after lunch, I half expected Noel to come up and take us out to tea, but we were lazy so Alice and I sat in comfy chairs and we were having a nice talk about ideals when we saw khaki pass the window. We

*flew, Alice giggling as usual, and making an awful row.
I peeped over the stairs to see if it was Noel, but no, a
strange voice, so I called down "is that you, Noel?" but I
heard a shy voice say to the maid, "Will you tell Mrs.
Chambers my name is Gibson", and it was Harold.*

*I ran down just as I was, two plaits and no stockings,
to welcome him. I hope he didn't think me a very
dreadful person. He was soon quite at home and I ran
up to change. After a while Evelyn and Alice came
down and we had a jolly time in front of the fire. Oh
Maude, he is a dear boy. We are all in love with him. In
some ways he reminds me most awfully of Wallace. The
forehead is alike too. My heart felt like breaking, he has
so many little ways like Wallace, but I am learning not
to show my feelings and keep smiling and bright no
matter what happens. Oh Maude, I miss him more every
day and life seems to hold nothing for me now. Some
days I hardly understand it at all. I will write and tell
Aunt Rose all about Harold. He is looking awfully well,
and brown, and thoroughly enjoyed himself. I loved to
hear him laugh. Also he eats well. I wish I had more
time to get nicer cakes for him. He stayed with us until 9
o'c. and then we both had to go as he was going up to
Scotland that night, and I had to come back here.*

*I just love my work here and it is most interesting.
Also I am getting on and everyone is awfully good to me.
I get up at 6 o'c. and breakfast is at 6:40. We come on
duty at 7 and have to hustle to get everything fixed and
ready for prayers at 8:30. After that I go round with
sister and watch, and help with all the dressings. I seem
to be always asking questions, but sister is awfully good
and explains everything to me and makes it most
interesting to watch. Last week I went up to my first
operation. I don't think I could have stood it if I hadn't*

*had ten minutes in my room just before I went up. I
think the feeling uppermost was pity. I knew it was being
done to make them better, so I tried to learn all I could.
But oh, it was awful the way they cut them about. After
a time, wonder came in to it. I thought what a
wonderful gift God has given to man, the power to make
others well, and oh, the patience of the men. They are so
bright and cheerful through it all and nearly always
grateful for all we do.*

*Some of our men are so nice. We have a lot of
Scotchmen — one, a Seaforth Highlander, MacDonald,
is such a dear boy — only 19. He's been here a year
now — his wounds won't heal. He has an angel face,
fair, curly hair, and blue-grey eyes, and his laugh, well
it's always ringing down the ward, and making us all
smile. Sometimes I have to tell him not to do things, then
he hides under the bed clothes and says I am horrid.
(He reminds me of Mac.) He had both feet blown away
and I fear I spoil him because he was a Seaforth.*

*At first I felt very tired in the evening, but now I take
my two hours off quietly, and it's ever so much better. I
feel ever so much better with this real work but my time
here is up 1st of March, and then I must sign on for a
year if I want to get into a real big military hospital.*

*I had a talk with Father, and said I want Nona to go
to a good boarding school. I think he is going to do it.*

*With ever so much love dear sister of mine,
Your loving little sister,
Cecie.*

Cecie Chambers (right), 1915

ORDER FORM

A LOVELY LETTER FROM CECIE

ALSO AVAILABLE FROM YOUR LOCAL BOOKSTORE

_____ Copies @ $19.95 (Cdn) each _____
Add 7% GST _____
Add $5.00 for first book for Shipping & Handling _____
Add $2.00 for each additional book for Shipping & Handling _____
Total enclosed _____

Make cheque or money order payable to:

JOHN GRAHAM GILLIS

Name _____

Address _____

City, Province/State _____

Postal/Zip Code _____

Phone (work) _____ (home) _____

John Graham Gillis
2092 Cliffwood Lane
North Vancouver, BC
Canada V7G 2A7
For more information call (604) 929-6842
e-mail: jgillis@axionet.com

Thank you for your order!